# Hand Appliqué
## by Machine

### Beth Ferrier

Applewood Farm
Publications

# Hand Appliqué
## by Machine

### Beth Ferrier

Along with Nathan, Jacob, Caleb and David, this book was produced by Beth and Kent Ferrier. Beth did all the writing, all of the quilts, helped with the photography and the computer formatting of the book. (In other words, all the fun stuff.) Kent did all the things that Beth doesn't like to do. The fact that he does them so well and with such a great sense of humor (even when presented with "the look") is why he is the best husband and friend in the whole entire world.

**Library of Congress Control Number: 2002094057**
Published in Saginaw, Michigan
**ISBN: 0-9714654-2-8**
**Printed in Canada**

Applewood Farm Publications
3655 Midland Road
Saginaw, MI 48603
989-799-6973
fax: 989-799-6974
www.applewoodfarmquilts.com
quilting@applewd.com

Hand Applique by Machine

# Introduction

A long time ago, when I was a brand new Quilter, I went to my first quilt show. All of the quilts that I truly adored were covered with appliqué. They were meticulously crafted, beautifully rendered, and so beyond my skill! I went back to my piecing, but appliqué was never far from my mind.

I will gladly admit that I am a recovering perfectionist, and a former handwork snob. (Real quilts are hand pieced, hand appliquéd and hand quilted. sniff!) After hand piecing and hand quilting my first quilt in 1975 I decided I'd had enough of hand piecing. I realized that I could make a pieced quilt with my sewing machine that looks just like the hand pieced quilt, and it wouldn't take a year to complete.

Next I learned that free motion quilting can look just like traditional hand quilting. I had the good luck to be taught basic free motion quilting by Diane Gaudynski, the queen of beautiful traditional style free motion quilting. Whoops, hand quilting became a thing of the past for me.

It wasn't long before I just couldn't stand avoiding appliqué any more. While I was sure that only quilting goddesses could needle-turn, I took a lot of classes in both hand and machine appliqué. I learned all kinds of hand appliqué methods, back basting, front basting, you name it, I tried it. I even learned how to needle-turn. I'm pretty good at it too, but terribly slow.

And then I stumbled upon blind hem machine appliqué. At long last I could have the look of handwork with the speed of my machine. Now I didn't invent this technique. It's been around forever. I've just made it easier. For the last seven years I have been refining the process to make producing machine appliqué that masquerades as handwork simple, quick and fun.

So come and play with me. Let's appliqué something!

# Chapter One

So if this is a book on appliqué, what am I doing in the office supply store?   Quilters have never hesitated to adapt household items for quilting tools.   We are going to be using some wacky stuff.  But please don't tell the quilt police. They will put it a quilty name on it and charge us three times as much!

## The tools of the technique:

- Awesome appliqué design and fabric
-  Photocopies of the appliqué design
- Reynold's Plastic Coated Freezer Paper, available in most grocery stores.  Look for it in the sandwich bag and plastic wrap department.  Totally Stable from Sulky, Inc. is a great substitute for freezer paper.
- Stapler and staple puller
- Scissors (dressmaker, 5" knife edge, pocket, appliqué, we'll get into the details later)
- Iron and ironing board
- Spray Sizing,  my preferred brand is Magic Sizing
- Glue sticks, water-soluble or for fabric.
- Cuticle sticks
- Flat flower head pins
- Sulky Polyester Invisible thread
- 100% cotton thread
- Sewing machine needles
- Sewing machine
- Terry bath towel
- Light box is handy but not required

## The Project: Five of Hearts

For each of the lessons in this book, I've designed a small project to illustrate the concepts. I'll be using the templates from those projects in the diagrams. For Chapter One, I've designed a simple little wreath of hearts to get us started with the basics in Hand Appliqué by Machine. The heart shape is an excellent shape to teach all the skills you need to appliqué anything. You'll find all the requirements and specific project directions in the project section, starting on page 69.

## Let's get started!

In appliqué often the first step is to make plastic templates. Not only does that take forever, no matter how carefully I trace, my lines are never as accurate as the original. I'm spending all this time (and money for the template plastic) for a not-so-great template that I will most likely only use once. We're going to skip this step. We will be using photocopies and freezer paper templates instead.

## Start with Photocopies

Remember that the scanner on your computer also acts as a copier.

Copiers also allow you to adjust the size of the motif.

We will need one freezer paper template for each part of the appliqué on the quilt. They can't be reused. One way to speed the process along is to cut multiple layers of freezer paper whenever we can. We can neatly cut up to six layers of freezer paper at one time. Any more than that and we risk having lousy templates. The freezer paper shapes are the most important part of getting excellent edges on our appliqué, so we want to take our time and get the best possible outcome.

Determine the number of repeats of a motif you will have in your project. Let's say, for example, you have 36 identical flowers in the border of your quilt. Remember that you can cut up to six layers of freezer paper at one time. That means you will need at least six photocopies of the flower shape to make 36 flowers.

Decide how many heart wreaths you want to make to determine how many photocopies you will need to make. I always make a couple more photocopies than the minimum required for myself. I like to make extra appliqué motifs so I can choose from the very best. That also lets me experiment with color placement. I can then choose from the very best shapes and toss the extra in the "orphaned appliqué" tin on my shelf.

Each one of the photocopied heart shapes and leaf shapes needs to be cut apart loosely. That means just chop the motifs apart, but don't cut on the line just yet.

Now let's take just a tiny detour and talk about copyright issues. As long as you are making photocopies for your personal use you are not infringing on anyone's rights. As soon as you make extra copies for your buddy because she likes the design but she doesn't want to buy the book then you are breaking copyright laws. Changing the size, the color of the appliqué, the arrangement or placing the motif in a new design does not make it yours. It will always be the designer's motif. But if it's just for private use, it's totally okay. If you enter your quilt in a show, please give the designer credit!

## Stack the Freezer Paper

Rip off three hunks of freezer paper. Make each sheet **about** 10" long. Fold these in **about** half and rip them apart on the fold. Please be messy **about** this! There is nothing magic **about** this size. It's just an easy size to work with. Don't be frugal. Freezer paper is cheap, your time isn't.

Make one stack of six layers of freezer paper, all plastic side up. Staple the stacks together in the corners. (It's okay to be messy about this, really!) We need to keep the plastic side up to have the finished appliqué look like the original. If we use the freezer paper with the paper side up the finished appliqué will be the mirror image of the original.

## Staple the Shapes

Now staple the heart and leaf shapes to the plastic side of the stack. Give yourself a couple of inches between the shapes. Don't fold or roll the stack of freezer paper to reach the shapes for stapling. Just staple the parts that you can get to at the moment.

Each shape needs a couple of staples. Make sure that the staples are all inside the lines. We are going to cut on the lines. The staples are tough on the scissors.

Sneak a staple into the sharp point of the heart. Use as many staples as you need to keep the layers from shifting. But don't get carried away, you'll have to take them right back out again.

Once you've stapled what you can reach chop apart the freezer paper stacks. Again, we are not yet cutting on the lines. As you open up the spaces around your shapes you can staple the areas you couldn't reach before.

## Cut out the Shapes

Now it's finally time to cut on the lines. And here is where my gadget addiction comes to light. I'm a firm believer in the right tool for the job. Our freezer paper shapes are the most important part of the Hand Appliqué by Machine technique. They need to be the best that we can make them. I use my very best scissors to cut the stacks of freezer paper.

I use Ginghers' 8" dressmaker scissors in this step. These heavy scissors are powerful for cutting through seven layers of paper. The long blades help me get a smooth cut. I use Ginghers because they are very sharp and they stay sharp. I've been using the same pair of scissors for at least four years and they are still sharp enough to cut both paper and fabric cleanly. (No, I am not on Gingher's payroll. ☺)

Besides having an excellent pair of scissors, moving the paper instead of the scissors as you cut will give you very accurate cuts. Turn the paper into the blades as you close the blades of the scissors.

It's a good idea to cut the freezer paper over a garbage can. Get rid of the scraps as you work. It's a real pain to be a petal short of a flower. And get rid of the photocopy layer. It can't be used again for cutting templates and it doesn't stick to the fabric.

## Adhere the freezer paper shapes

Now it's time to fire up your iron. I always keep my iron set on scorch. We do not want steam, it wrinkles the freezer paper we just worked so hard to keep neat.

Choose the fabric you want to use for the hearts and leaves. I suggest that you make a couple of extra shapes for practice.

Place the shiny side of the paper on the **wrong** side of the desired fabric and press in place with the hot iron. Be sure to leave at least an inch around each shape.

## Add the seam allowance

Cut the pieces loosely out of the fabric. Just as with the paper cutting, we are going to separate the shapes before we try to cut accurate seam allowances. It's very awkward to handle large pieces of fabric, especially when we are trying to be neat.

Once the shapes are separated out, trim the fabric around the freezer paper ADDING about a ¼" seam allowance. It is better to cut too large a seam allowance and need to trim it later than to cut too narrow a seam allowance and have it fray away as you baste it. Beginners should aim for a heaping ¼", with practice, go for the scant ¼" seam allowance.

I have another pair of scissors that I like to use for this part. The 5" knife-edge scissors are much lighter weight than the large dressmaker scissors that I use for cutting the paper. When I'm working on a large project I can be trimming appliqués for a long time. Using lighter weight scissors protects my hands from fatigue. (I warned you about my gadget addiction!)

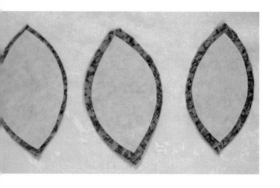

Notice the seam allowances in the three leaves? One is too skinny, one is too fat and one is just right!

## Clipping the curves

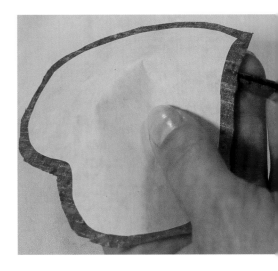

While we are trimming the seam allowances, we need to clip some of the trouble areas. One clip in the seam allowance at the cleavage will give you a sharp "v". I like to clip within a few threads of the freezer paper, not all the way to the paper. Leaving a few threads of seam allowance helps to prevent fraying.

Several clips in the inside curve of the side of the heart will give you a smooth curve in the finished appliqué. It is not necessary to clip outside curves.

Finally, trim the excess seam allowance fabric from the point of the heart and the ends of the leaves. Leave a scant ¼" seam allowance at the end of the point. I call this mitering the point, you'll see why when we basted it.

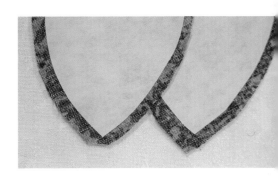

## The science of the glue stick

We will use a glue stick to paste the seam allowances to the freezer paper. This will hold them in place until we are done sewing them.

Not just any glue stick will do. It is important that the glue is water-soluble. It's also important that the glue is slimy. It needs to stick immediately to hold the seam allowance, but remain slippery for a few minutes so we can adjust the seam allowance.

Most brands will work just fine. The fabric glue sticks that we can get at our quilt shops or chain fabric stores will work great. The fabric glue sticks tend to be a little more expensive (and we can expect to use lots of them on a large appliqué project) and sometimes they are dried out.

Manufacturers keep messing about with their formulas, so don't be afraid to try new brands. My long time favorite glue stick company just changed the recipe, now the glue doesn't catch on the first fold. That glue stick brand is so outta here!

The gluing process can get messy, so you'll want to protect your work surface. I like to use a reversible pressing/cutting board for glue basting. The small size fits nicely in my lap. The pressing side is comfortable and the cutting side makes a perfect lap table. When it gets gobbed up with glue I simply spray it with cool water, let it sit for a few minutes and then scrap the glue off the cutting board surface.

The pressing/cutting board also makes this step very portable. I can take my rough-cut appliqué pieces, my 5" scissors and glue sticks and go sit on the porch swing. There I can baste my heart out; listening to the birds sing and watching for humming birds as they visit the garden.

## Glue basting the seam allowance

Now, let's baste these puppies. We'll start with the leaves.

First smear a little glue on the points of the leaves. Carefully, using the side of your thumb, fold the seam allowance over the point. Be very careful not to overwhelm the point. If you break the freezer paper point it will make it harder to get a sharp point. Go ahead and fold back the seam allowance on both ends of the leaves.

Hand Applique by Machine

Reapply the glue, this time all the way around the shape. The goal is to get most of the glue on the fabric seam allowance, and some on the edge of the freezer paper. Don't worry, this isn't rocket science. We want to apply a good amount of glue, don't be too skimpy, but we also don't want gobs of glue.

Moving clockwise around the shape, pinch the seam allowance to fold it over the freezer paper. Use the side of your thumb. You'll be able to feel the edge of the freezer paper. Don't worry about making it perfect right now. We'll dress it up in a minute. Just get it tacked down about every ¼" all the way around.

## The art of the cuticle stick

Once the seam allowance is tacked in place its time to make adjustments. Flip the appliqué shape right side up and take a hard look at it. Is it as good as it can be? Are the edges smooth and lovely? If not, all is not lost. This is why we like slimy glue sticks. The right leaf in the picture is a victim of "the pokies".

I like to use a cuticle stick to coax those edges into perfection. Flip the appliqué back to the wrong side and use your fingernail or a cuticle stick to smooth the seam allowance. The folds in the seam allowances on the wrong side of the shape are only important if they are making a pokie on the right side. If the fold doesn't make a pokie, leave it alone.

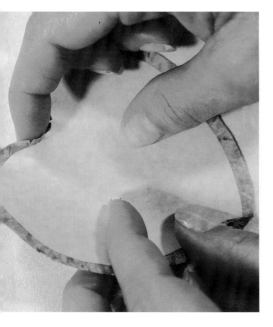

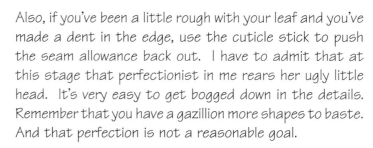

Also, if you've been a little rough with your leaf and you've made a dent in the edge, use the cuticle stick to push the seam allowance back out. I have to admit that at this stage that perfectionist in me rears her ugly little head. It's very easy to get bogged down in the details. Remember that you have a gazillion more shapes to baste. And that perfection is not a reasonable goal.

The points can also be adjusted so that they are totally excellent. It's okay to overlap the seam allowances if that is what's needed to get a super sharp point that the quilt police will envy.

## Baste the Heart

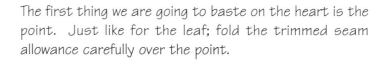

The first thing we are going to baste on the heart is the point. Just like for the leaf; fold the trimmed seam allowance carefully over the point.

The other area in need of special attention is the cleavage. A single clip into the notch of the "v" will give a sharp cleavage. I like to clip within a few threads of the freezer paper. That gives me a little bit of an edge to turn.

Start by applying glue from about an inch on both sides of the cleavage. Working from the wrong side, drag your index finger through the cleavage, sticking the seam allowance down to the freezer paper. Don't worry if it's not just right just yet, we'll fix it in a minute.

Apply glue to the rest of the heart and tack baste the entire shape. Now go back with the cuticle stick or your fingernail and adjust all the seam allowances. You can even slide the cleavage seam allowance to the side to increase the sharpness of the point.

The clips in the inside curve edge of the heart should have made turning that edge very easy. Again, I like to clip the seam allowance within a couple of threads of the freezer paper. That leaves a few threads to turn, reducing the opportunity for "fuzzies", threads that have a mind of their own.

## Going in Circles

To complete the heart design, we need to baste the center circle. The hardest part of getting a perfect circle is cutting a perfect circle out of freezer paper. So I don't!

Finding the best template for circles takes us back to the office supply store. Check out the sticky label department. We can find circles as small as ¼" up to 2" or more! These make excellent templates for appliqué.

Stick the circle to your clothes a couple of times before you stick it on the wrong side of your fabric. Without that step, the circles are harder to get back out of the appliqué. (Yes, all the freezer paper does leave the project before we're done!) I used 1" mailing seal labels for my circles.

Trim the seam allowance a little narrower on a circle than you would for other motifs. That will leave less bulk to turn to the wrong side.

If you wish to draw your own circles and cut them from freezer paper I recommend buying a circle template at the office supply or craft store. It's much easier to draw inside a curve than outside.

When cutting, be sure to turn the paper into the scissors. Consider cutting fewer layers at a time.

## Tune Up The Machine

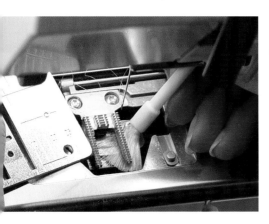

Let's get those sewing machines fired up and ready to sew. We depend on our machines to make the small, fine stitches that others achieve by hand. Every machine needs regular maintenance to perform at peak levels. Drag out your machine's manual and check out what kind of chores you should be regularly performing. At the very least you need to remove the throat plate and clean the lint out the area around the feed dogs and bobbin case. There should not be a felt pad under the feed dogs!

Some machines like to be oiled. Others do not. Check with the manual or a sewing machine mechanic to see if your machine needs regular oiling.

Speaking of sewing machine mechanics, your machine should see one regularly! Once a year is usually often enough. Think of it as a well baby visit. Your machine will hum along so happily and you will spend less time creating "blue air" when the machine malfunctions.

# Bobbin Along

And while you have the manual out, review the correct technique for filling a bobbin. It's easy to loose track of a thread guide, forget a little twist here or there. A well-filled bobbin really will improve the quality of the stitches.

For hand appliqué by machine I use a good quality 100% cotton thread in a neutral color that matches the background fabric of the appliqué project. I prefer to use a 50-weight thread, which is the normal sewing weight cotton. A finer thread can produce a looser tension in the bobbin and thereby find it's way to the right side of the appliqué. That is not the look we are after.

# Needle Little Love!

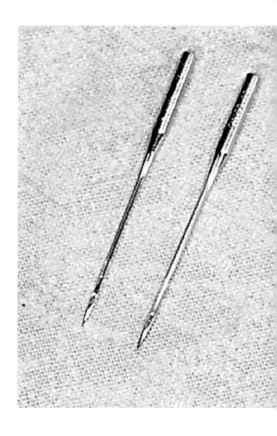

We have cleaned our machines, properly wound a couple of bobbins, now it is time for a new needle. Just as in hand appliqué, using the right sewing machine needle will insure an invisible stitch.

The best needle for this job is a 70/10 Sharp. The 70 is the European term for the size, the 10 is the English size. A 70/10 needle is finer than an 80/12, the size considered standard for basic sewing.

The "Sharp" refers to the shape of the needle's point. Believe it or not, universal needles are not sharp. They are slightly ball pointed so that they can be used on a variety of projects. We are going to be stitching through three layers of fabric and one layer of freezer paper. We want a very sharp point that can easily plow through all of those layers. (Some brands use the term Microtex instead of Sharp. It's the same idea.)

Use the very best quality needles that you can afford. Needles really *do* make a very big difference in the quality of the stitch.

It is also recommended that you change the needle every 6-8 hours of stitching time. I change mine more often. Sewing through freezer paper with its layer of plastic and glue and fabric can be kind of rough on a needle.

## Invisible Thread

Invisible (monofilament) thread can be a controversial item. Since its introduction many years ago there have been dire predictions of disintegrating quilts, quilting stitches popping before our very eyes, appliqués falling off our quilts.

I have been using invisible thread for at least twelve years. Quilts that I quilted with invisible thread are still in daily use by my boys. Yes, they are worse for wear, but it's not from the invisible thread.

I'm wondering if invisible thread, which is made of nylon or polyester, is so fragile, why are our landfills full of nylon and polyester stuff that doesn't degrade?

Heat is the greatest enemy for our quilts, and tumbling in the dryer is really hard on all of the ingredients of a quilt. To increase the life of my utility quilts (which is really all of my quilts, even the ones for books and magazines), they are washed in cool water and dried on the clothesline. It's hard to beat the incredible fresh smell of a quilt dried on the line. It's one of my favorite things.

Anyway! I do recommend that you stick with the best quality invisible thread. It is finer and more flexible than the cheap stuff. Sewing machines sometimes have fits over invisible thread. The cheap stuff is usually the culprit. Sulky International makes the brand I prefer. It's polyester, not nylon. The spool fits neatly on all machines. It sews up like a dream and rarely gives my students' machines trouble.

Invisible thread comes in both clear and smoke colors. Match the color of the thread to the color of the background. Generally, clear invisible thread is used on light to medium color fabrics. The smoke invisible thread is used on medium to dark fabrics.

Sometimes the clear thread glistens on dark fabric. And using smoke thread on fabric that is too light will give the appearance of a permanent pencil line. It's important to test. I've been surprised at times by what turns out to be the appropriate thread.

We love invisible thread because we can't see it. And we curse invisible thread because we can't see it. To more easily thread the needle put a small piece of white paper behind the eye of the needle. That will help you see the eye. Good luck! And remember there are 440 yards of thread on the spool. If you were doing hand appliqué you would be rethreading a tiny eye in a tiny needle every 18 inches!

## The Best Foot Forward

It's helpful to have what is called an open toed embroidery foot for your sewing machine. This will allow you to clearly see the needle and watch the stitch as it is formed.

# The Stitch

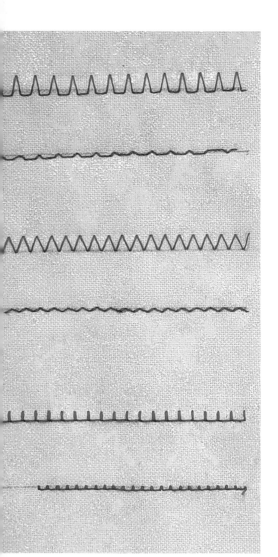

The secret to totally invisible machine appliqué stitches is finding the best stitch on our machine. Our first choice is a stitch called the blind-hem stitch. The stitch looks like a drunken straight stitch. It is comprised of a series of straight stitches interrupted by a zig and a zag.

If you have a fancy machine, look for the blind-hem stitch in the first menu of stitches. It is often found with the utility stitches.

We need to make this stitch very narrow and very small. On my sewing machine, a Bernina 1530, the stitch width is set for .75 mm and the length is set at 1 mm. Each machine is different so you'll need to test to get the very best setting.

When first beginning, set the width just at a little more generous width. That is more forgiving, you'll be less likely to miss the edge of the appliqué. As you have more practice, you'll be able to narrow the stitch and get truly invisible stitches.

Some machines have an option of having the needle end in the fabric every time you stop stitching. This "needle down" option is a wonderful thing. (It was one of the features at the top of my list when I bought my first Bernina back in 1990.) Ending with the needle in the fabric will hold the work in exactly the place where you stopped. It will give you pinpoint control, allowing you to readjust the work without losing your place.

Some machines without the needle down option can be adjusted by a sewing machine repair person to always stop with the needle down. You will need to turn the handwheel to release the project when you've finished stitching, but this is way easier than having to turn the handwheel for needle down for each adjustment you need to make.

## Uh-oh

Sometimes we find we have a machine that just doesn't want to play nice. Some sewing machines don't have a blind-hem stitch, and worse, some machines won't let you adjust the size of the stitch. So close and yet so very far!

But don't despair. Some machines can be fooled into co-operating. If your machine has a blind-hem stitch but won't let you adjust the size look for what is called a twin (or double) needle limiter. This little function restricts the width of the stitch to protect the extra width of a twin (double) needle. The icon looks like a little tuning fork. This function is especially useful on Pfaff sewing machines. Engage the stitch function, engage the twin needle limiter and then test for the right width stitch.

Some machines will allow you to draw your own stitch. My preference would be three straight stitches, a zig and a zag.

Here are alternate stitches that can be used quite successfully. The blanket stitch is a great alternative. Instead of a zig and zag, the bite is straight over and back. Often this stitch can be adjusted even when the blind-hem stitch can't.

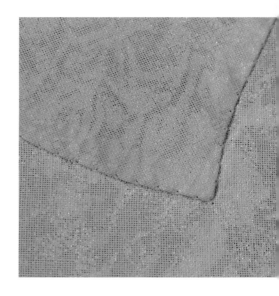

We can also use the basic zigzag on the machine. As always, you will need to test the stitch to find the best settings for your machine. We are looking for a little longer length (we DON'T want a satin stitch!), and a narrow width.

In the samples shown at right one is done with the blind hem stitch and one is done with the zig zag. Can you tell the difference? Neither could we!

## Weasel Words

I sure wish that I could know everything about every machine so I could just tell you how to set your machine. There are just too many machines out there with new machines appearing almost every day.

Please be sure to read your manual. The shop where you bought your machine should be an excellent source for help in getting the most out of your machine.

If you decide its time for a new machine you don't have to spend a million buckeronis on a top-of-the-line computerized machine to achieve gorgeous Hand Appliqué by Machine. (Unless of course you're looking for an excuse to, and then it would be imperative that you have the very latest, greatest, glow-in-the-dark model out there!)

Consider buying a previously loved machine. That's a great way to get the most machine for the smallest investment. That first Bernina I bought was a used machine. I am still using that machine on a daily basis.

And if you are considering a new machine, the most important factor is the dealer. I will admit to a bias towards Bernina. I just love mine (all five of them!). But most of the machines out there sold by independent shops are totally excellent machines. It doesn't matter how great the machine is if you can't stand the dealer. You are going to need to spend a good deal of time with this shop to get the most out of your machine.

## Tension Adjustments

Once the stitch is the right size we need to test for tension settings. Test drive your stitch on a small scrap of fabric folded to make several layers of fabric. Don't bother trying to stitch along an edge, just stitch out a line on the scrap. (You will not get a good indication of tension settings on just a single layer of fabric. I guarantee that it will look scary on just one layer.)

Take a good look at the stitching line. We don't want to see any bobbin thread on the top. If the bobbin thread is showing on the top it's time to adjust the tension. Start by loosening the top tension. Just a tick or two is usually enough. (Loosen = lower, that's the best way to remember, to loosen the tension, lower the number.)

If that doesn't work, we may have to tighten the bobbin tension. (It will be okay, really!) It is very simple if you have a drop-out bobbin case. You will find a small screw on the side of the case. Turn the slot of the screw ¼ turn to the right (lefty=loosey, righty=tighty) to tighten.

You can tell if your bobbin case is adjusted properly if you can hold the bobbin thread and the bobbin case is suspended in the air. Now just give it a little yank. Does the bobbin case drop an inch or two? If it does, it's just right. If it doesn't move, it's too tight. If it falls on the floor, it's waaaay too loose.

If you have a drop-in bobbin you will need to read the manual or consult your sewing machine dealer for help.

Good grief! It's taken a bazillion pages to get to this point. But for me this is one of the best parts of Hand Appliqué by Machine. Up until now the process is as portable as any hand appliqué method out there.

It's rather like planning a wedding. We dream and plan and prepare for sometimes years in advance and then ta-da! It's over in a day! Hand Appliqué by Machine is like that. The preparation is what takes the time. The sewing is done rather quickly.

## Prepare the background

Choose the background fabric you would like to use for your project. We're going to get crazy with backgrounds in Chapter 5. For now, an 18" square of fabric is just the right size. Press the background fabric carefully. I like to use lots of spray sizing to keep the background crisp. Gently fold the background right sides together to mark the center.

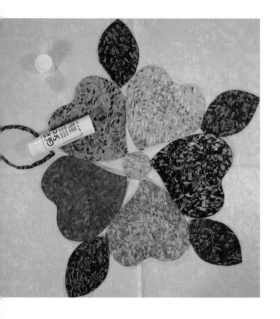

Smear a generous layer of glue on the wrong side of the basted circle and stick it right in the center of the background. Repeat the process with each of the basted hearts. You may wish to "dry fit" the appliqués before you glue them down. ("Dry fit" is what you do with floor tile. You lay it down and test the layout before you paste it down.) Finally, when you are happy with the layout, paste those shapes in place.

It is useful to pin the appliqués in place as well. Sometimes as the piece is stitched the placement basting works loose. A couple of flat flower head pins will hold the shapes in place without distorting the freezer paper template.

## It's finally time to sew!

Using the Five of Hearts project as my example, I'd start my sewing in the center with the circle. As we begin to stitch we want the straight stitch part to fall totally on the background fabric. But we need to be so close to the appliqué that the side of the needle brushes the folded edge of the appliqué but doesn't pierce it. The fine 70/10 Sharp needle allows us to get very close to the edge of the appliqué.

Go slowly now, the zig zag part of the stitch will bite into the folded edge of the appliqué. That is exactly what we want. As you practice it will become easier to keep the straight part of the stitch in just the right place. Suddenly it will seem like your "bite" has become huge. You are in the groove now! It's time to narrow the stitch width just a tick. Keep doing this until the "bite" just barely catches the fold of the threads and you can do this consistently without missing. Ah, isn't excellence exhilarating?

Hand Applique by Machine

For those of you using a modified zigzag, the placement of the stitch is a little different. You will try to keep the bulk of the stitch **on** the appliqué with the zig to the right just falling off of the appliqué. It's very helpful if you can move the sewing machine needle position all the way to the right. The inside edge of the sewing machine foot can then help you stay in place.

Circles are tough because you have to keep readjusting the machine. But it's worth the work because excellent circles are the hallmark of fabulous appliqué. The appliqué police will be green with envy.

Okay, the circle was obvious. Let's consider the easiest path for our next line of stitching. Notice how the heart points make sort of a little curvy star around the circle? Let's stitch that part.

Be careful to really nail down the point of the heart. You can very gently "hold back" the appliqué, forcing the machine to stitch in place until the "bite" catches that point. I try to nail a "bite" on each side and exactly on the end. We worked so hard to baste those points so they were sharp to the molecule, now is not the time to get sloppy!

Finally, let's cruise around the outside of the hearts. We can even catch the leaves on this pass! How cool is that!

As you stitch, keep your hands flat on the fabric, forming a triangle with your thumbs and index fingers. Keep the background fabric flat and taut, but don't stretch it. It will take a little practice. You'll know you've arrived when the background square is the same size as you cut it after all the appliqué is done.

Don't worry about the holes left by the needle. The glue is holding them open. They will close as we continue the process. Honest they do.

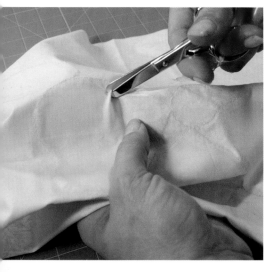

# Remove the Background

This is where some hand-appliquists get their knickers in a twist. We just love a good controversy, don't we? We're going to cut the background fabric away from the appliqués. We need to get the freezer paper out of there. Some folks like to say that cutting the background away causes the appliqué to sink. I feel that it's just the opposite. To me, layer upon layer of appliqué looks like a bad case of appliqué build-up! When the background layers are cut away it allows the appliqué to appear as one beautifully shaded unit.

So let's take that background away. Cut the background fabric away from behind the appliqué motifs, leaving a quarter-inch seam allowance. Be neat doing this. The seam allowance can show through just as it does for our piecing. We can use that to our advantage when it's time for quilting this puppy.

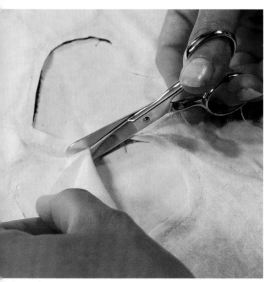

I like to use pocket scissors for this. (Yes, another gadget.) They look like kindergarten scissors, but they are very sharp. They were designed for heirloom sewing; the blunt end doesn't catch in the pricey French insertion lace as you cut the batiste away. Pocket scissors let us cut the background away without worry of chopping through the appliqué.

## The hard way

Occasionally I will have a student who just balks at using my special magic trick to remove the paper. It is possible to remove the paper without the trick; it's just not very fun. To prove the point, I spent 4 days removing the paper the hard way from the appliqué of Peaceful Garden Path, a queen size quilt that appeared in my first book, *Out of the Cupboard and Onto the Bed*. I could have done it in an afternoon if I had used the magic trick. But no, I had to prove that there was another way to remove the paper.

To remove the freezer paper the hard way, tear the template down the middle and roll the paper away from the seam allowance. You don't want to just pull the paper away. It will come out, but it may also fray away the appliqué's seam allowance and even pop stitches.

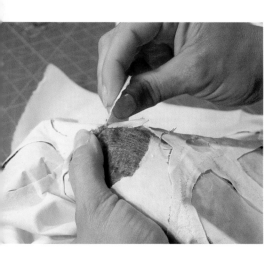

# The Magic Trick

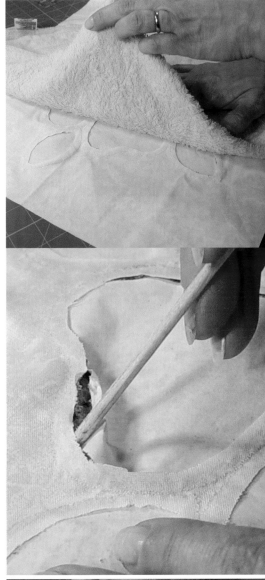

Now that you've suffered through the hard way of removing the freezer paper, it's time for a little magic.

Moisten a terry towel and lay it on the wrong side of the appliqué. We don't want this towel to be dripping wet, just good and damp. With four teenaged boys at home for the summer and holidays, I can usually find one that is just right on the bathroom floor.

Pat the towel down on the back of the appliqué. That will make good contact between the towel and the seam allowances. That's where we want the moisture to go. Let the towel and appliqué sit for a few minutes, 15 to 20 is about what it usually all that it takes.

This little bit of moisture will soften the glue making the paper removal a piece of cake! Once the applique is damp the freezer paper shapes will just slide out of the work. You can use a cuticle stick to lift any seam allowances that are playing stubborn.

If the paper isn't coming out easily, reapply the towel for a few minutes more.

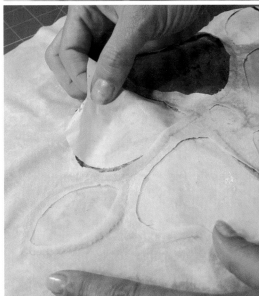

If you slathered a ton of glue on the backs of the appliqués to hold them in place for stitching this could be a messy job. Keep the damp towel nearby to wipe your hands. But it's not so bad because you know that you are almost done!

People always worry that their fabric will run if wet. I've been using this technique for years. I never prewash my fabric and I have never had color run!

## Dry this Puppy

We do NOT want our appliqué sitting around wet. It doesn't matter if you've prewashed your fabric or not, if left to air dry there is always a risk of colors migrating.

Once all of the paper is removed, quick like a bunny, go to that iron set on scorch and carefully press the appliqué. I like to use spray sizing on the appliqué as well. I find it much easier to work with crisp fabrics than wimpy ones. My machine quilting goes much better if the piece is as flat as can be.

## And hey, its an applique

Trim the appliqué to the desired size. Look what you did! Isn't it beautiful?!

## Isn't it lovely?

I suffer from terminal practicality. Even though in my heart of hearts I am a person who enjoys the process, I do sort of like to have a product when I'm finally all done. It was all I could do to keep from making a bazillion squares and turning them into a queen sized quilt. So I made pillows out of my Five of Heart samples. The round pillow started out as an 18" square; I just trimmed to corners off.

Remember to check out the project section of the book for all the supplies needed to make your very own Five of Hearts design. If you do make a queen sized quilt with the design would you please send me a picture?

## It's My Story and I'm Sticking With It

I give you permission to be done when the appliqué is done. You don't have to make it into anything. In fact, I think you should tuck it away in a drawer, maybe even put a date on it. When you find it again in a year or so you'll be able to celebrate just how much your skill has improved in so short a time!

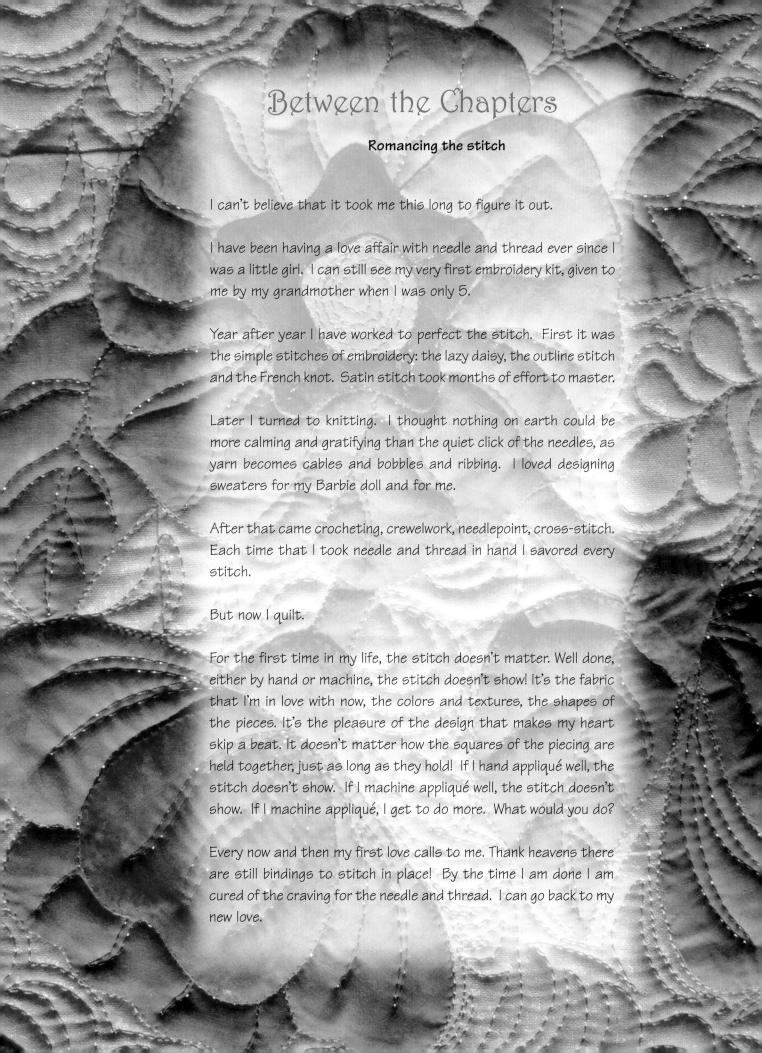

# Between the Chapters

### Romancing the stitch

I can't believe that it took me this long to figure it out.

I have been having a love affair with needle and thread ever since I was a little girl. I can still see my very first embroidery kit, given to me by my grandmother when I was only 5.

Year after year I have worked to perfect the stitch. First it was the simple stitches of embroidery: the lazy daisy, the outline stitch and the French knot. Satin stitch took months of effort to master.

Later I turned to knitting. I thought nothing on earth could be more calming and gratifying than the quiet click of the needles, as yarn becomes cables and bobbles and ribbing. I loved designing sweaters for my Barbie doll and for me.

After that came crocheting, crewelwork, needlepoint, cross-stitch. Each time that I took needle and thread in hand I savored every stitch.

But now I quilt.

For the first time in my life, the stitch doesn't matter. Well done, either by hand or machine, the stitch doesn't show! It's the fabric that I'm in love with now, the colors and textures, the shapes of the pieces. It's the pleasure of the design that makes my heart skip a beat. It doesn't matter how the squares of the piecing are held together, just as long as they hold! If I hand appliqué well, the stitch doesn't show. If I machine appliqué well, the stitch doesn't show. If I machine appliqué, I get to do more. What would you do?

Every now and then my first love calls to me. Thank heavens there are still bindings to stitch in place! By the time I am done I am cured of the craving for the needle and thread. I can go back to my new love.

# Chapter Two

Now that we've mastered the basics, let's take this baby out on the road and see what she can do!

We aren't limited to simple appliqué outlines. The real beauty of this technique is how easily we can master complex shapes. Let's sneak up on this by starting with a two-part shape. To illustrate, I'll be using the templates for the pears and leaves from the project No Partridges in This Pear Tree. You can find all the details for the quilt in the project section, page 74.

## Templates for Compound Shapes

We'll work through the steps of Chapter One, adding some new details as we go.

This time we're going to fold the freezer paper so that we can make mirror image shapes. Pull a good-sized

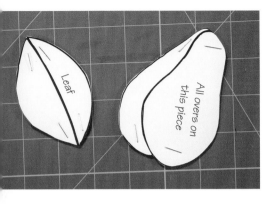

chunk of freezer paper out of the box. Fold it in half, plastic sides together. Now fold this chunk into thirds. Don't spend a lot of time agonizing over this. You don't get any extra points if your stack is neatly folded! Put a staple or two around the edges to hold the stack together. This will give us 6 layers of freezer paper (the magic number!).

Staple the pear and leaf photocopies to the freezer paper stacks. Put staples inside each half of each shape. Don't cut them apart yet! Just cut out the outline of the pair and the leaf.

Once the whole shapes are cut out we can turn to the internal cuts. Let's work on one motif at a time, we'll start with one of the leaves.

Cut the two halves of one of the leaves apart. Carefully remove the staples from one of the halves. Try not to disturb the layers of freezer paper as you remove the staples.

Toss away the photocopy. It's done its job, retire it. Now label the top freezer paper shape #1. The next shape should be plastic side up, flip that over and write a 2 on the paper side. Next comes shape #3, flip over the next one and label that #4 finish up by labeling layers 5 and 6.

Now turn to the other half of the leaf. Take the staples out, toss the photocopy layer. Label these guys just exactly the same way as the other half. Start with #1, finish with #6. Put the pieces labeled 1 together in a stack. These two pieces will make a leaf. Repeat that with all the leaf pieces you cut. When I'm making tons of shapes, I staple all of the freezer paper templates for each motif together. In this case I would have six sets of two templates for my leaves.

Hand Applique by Machine

Continue with each of the leaf sets. The next group of leaf templates would be labeled starting with number 7, finishing with 12. The goal is to have each set of freezer paper templates have its very own number. Repeat the process until you have enough leaf and pear templates to make the topiary of your dreams.

I know you're thinking that I've gone over the edge. A little obsessive-compulsive disorder in my history, eh? But there really is a good reason for doing this. We are going to have to bring the halves of the leaves back together again to make a complete leaf. That means that we'll want to align those templates right along the centerline that we cut. By bringing back together the same layer of freezer paper in each shape we are guaranteed a perfect fit, every time! Just wait until we get to the more complex shapes. You'll be glad that you humored me.

## A Word about Mirror Images

Notice that all of the even numbered templates were plastic side up. These will end up looking slightly different from the odd numbered template motifs. Making mirror image shapes is a sneaky way to add complexity to a design. Left-facing motifs register in the brain as different motifs from right-facing motifs. Even if the designer didn't think of it, you can add this complexity to any design.

But trying to fit left-facing templates into a right-facing motif is about as much fun as trying to get the Congress of the United States to cooperate. (And about as successful.) This is one of the reasons we take the time to label the freezer paper shapes. Keeping them organized will prevent a lot of weeping and gnashing of teeth and beating of breast later on. Nothing is sadder than being a petal short of a flower.

# The value of value

Another advantage of grouping all of the templates for each motif arises when you begin to work with the fabric. As you decide what fabric to use for each piece you can consider the whole shape.

Appliquists often try to create dimension in their motifs using the print of the fabric. Mottled fabrics make this easier for us. Working with the shape as a whole allows us to take the fullest advantage of the fabric.

Take a good look at my topiary. By carefully choosing value placement I was able to suggest a light source coming from the top right. Notice how the leaves and pears are of lighter fabrics in the upper right, darker fabrics show up in the lower left.

Even the individual shapes have depth because of value placement. There is a saying in the quilt world: **Value does all the work and color gets all the credit.** (I don't know who said it first, but I think she's a genius and I'd like to thank her.)

Value refers to the intensity or saturation of color. We often refer to it as a shade of a color, but that is technically not correct. A shade is a color with black added. A tone is a color with white added. The value is the depth, the range of intensity of the same color.

Value is relative. A fabric may be the dark one in a collection of light fabrics and also the light one in a collection of dark fabrics. Notice how the medium value center bar in the diagram changes from dark to light without changing value.

When a Quilter masters the concept of value, color becomes irrelevant. Great quilts are a combination of light, medium and dark. Just as in life, without the dark, light has no meaning. And quilts that stay with the happy medium are as boring as they are safe.

Hand Applique by Machine

When looking for subtle changes in value consider using the other side of the fabric as the right side. "Wrong side" is rather shortsighted, don't you think? It very well may be just the perfect fabric for your design.

Back to the project. Adhere the freezer paper templates to the fabric. Play around with your fabrics, make some of the pears and leaves using lighter fabrics, some using darker fabric. This is where making extra templates comes in handy. You have more choices when it comes to laying out the appliqué on the background.

Cut the shapes out, adding a ¼" seam allowance.

## Overs and Unders

When it comes to basting compound shapes we have to do a little planning. Some shapes will be completely basted; most shapes will have some of the seam allowance left unbasted.

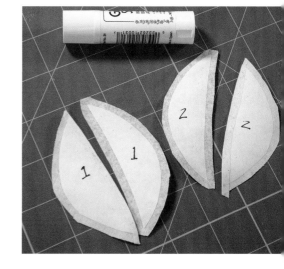

We have to decide which seam allowances of each shape are in front of other seam allowances. I call these "over" edges. Seam allowances that are left unbasted are called "unders".

The seam allowance of an "over" edge appears closer than an "under". It often takes trial and error to decide which seam allowance is an "over", which belongs "under". It will become easier with practice.

For the leaves, I made the lighter fabric of the two in the leaf the "over" edge. For the pear the larger shape was always the "over".

Working with the shapes for one of the leaves, baste only the centerline seam allowance that you want for the "over" edge.

# Docking

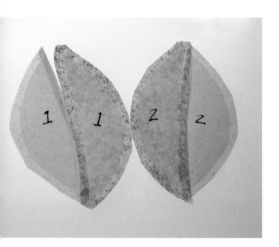

This is where we are going to bring the freezer paper templates back together to make a beautiful shape. I refer to this step as docking. It's sort of like how the space shuttle lines up with the space station.

Let's continue with the leaf shapes that have the center seam allowance basted. Smear a generous layer of glue stick paste on the basted seam allowance. Hold this shape up to a light source. Now hold the other piece of the leaf up to the light source along side the first piece. Notice how you can see through the unbasted ("under") center seam allowance.

Bring the leaf halves together, overlapping the "under" seam allowance with the basted "over" seam allowance. Continue to bring these pieces together until you can no longer see light through the seam allowance between the pieces. When you are happy with the positioning of the pieces, press the seam allowances together. The glue will hold them in place until you are ready to sew.

To finish the leaf, glue baste the outside seam allowance of the leaf. Start by folding the seam allowance over each end of the points on the leaf; continue basting around the outside edge of the shape, adjusting with that wonderful cuticle stick as needed.

When I started working out this technique I just used the light from a window or lamp to see through the seam allowance. Recently I've begun using a light box. I can even place a key for the shape on the light box and still have enough light to see through the seam allowance.

Hand Applique by Machine

## Stitch the interior seams

When all of the motifs are glue basted and docked its time to sew all of the interior seams. Start by test-stitching a line of the adjusted stitch on scraps of your appliqué fabric to check the tension and determine which thread color (smoke or clear) is the most invisible. Remember to stitch through multiple layers to get the most accurate reading of your tension.

It's a good idea to let the glue dry before you try to stitch the seams. (This is one of the advantages of making eleventy million motifs.) Wet glue will sometimes gum up the sewing machine needle. If you have an appliqué emergency, you can quickly dry the glue with a heavy-handed pressing with a hot iron.

Indeed, sometimes it's useful to press the appliqué shapes before stitching the interior seams. The freezer paper sometimes loosens in the basting process. A nice, hard pressing will totally flatten the appliqué making it easier to catch the folded edge of the appliqué all the way around the first time.

Just a reminder, the straight part of the stitch in on the background, needle so close to the turned edge that it brushes the edge but doesn't pierce it, the zig zag bite catches just a few threads of the edge.

## Design Freedom

We now have complete pears and leaves to arrange as we please on the background.

How many times while hand appliquéing have you stitched merrily around a shape only to find that it has shifted in the process and will not reach to cover the seam allowance it was supposed to cover. (I'm pretty sure that's why you see ladybugs embroidered on so many leaves.) When we work with completed motifs this will never happen! All of the seam allowances are handled before you even go to the background.

Working with complete motifs gives us complete design freedom. We can feel free to overlap or rearrange the components as we please. You can make your topiary just exactly like mine, or you can make more pears, or more leaves, or make it bigger or maybe even substitute flowers for the pears.......

## And if that's not enough

Any time you are working with a commercial design you can add your own flourishes. If the design is fairly simple, say for example, the Five of Hearts design of Chapter One, consider adding interest and dimension by cutting templates apart. A simple, flat leaf can suddenly turn in the wind with a single curved cut down the center.

Another little copyright issue here. Just because you were more clever than the designer and made a simple design more complex it doesn't make it yours. Consider it this way: you play a song from a piece of sheet music on the piano and you add lots of grace notes in between the printed notes. That doesn't make it your song, it makes it your arrangement of someone else's song.

As always, if you are making stuff for your own personal use copyright is no big deal. Just be mindful to get permission before you decide to sell a quilt from someone else's design or submit the quilt for publication.

# Between the chapters

## On Perfection

It's true; I'm a recovering perfectionist. I used to pray for release from perfectionism. God gave me four attention-deficit hyperactive boys to cure me. Be careful what you pray for, God has an incredible sense of humor.

It was easy to keep a perfect home when the boys were babies. During their naps I would diligently sort their wooden blocks by shape and color. Their books would be arranged by author and in number order if the publisher had the foresight. The Fisher-Price family would stand at attention, their home as neat as mine.

My spices were arranged in alphabetical order. The cereals were all safely stored in color-coded plastic dispenser boxes. My floors glowed, the end tables gleamed, the windows sparkled and all was right in my world.

And then we moved into a brand-new house. A beautiful house with light color carpet and newly painted white walls, surrounded by a sea of mud. One day shortly after we moved in one of my little darlings traipsed up the stairs leaving muddy shoe prints on the carpeted stairs and muddy handprints on the walls on **both sides** of the stairs.

I sat myself down on the top step and had a good cry. Lord, I prayed, did you really have to give me this beautiful house to cure me? He spoke quietly to my heart of hearts. It will clean up, He said, he will grow up, He said. You must love him now, you will have your perfect house later and it will make you lonely for that messy boy.

Everything changed that day, I became a recovering perfectionist. I learned how to smile and say; it'll clean up. Good enough makes me very happy. Mistakes are learning opportunities.

Think about the beautiful old antique quilts that we treasure. It is their character that we cherish, not their perfection. I can just hear its creator, as she discovers the one block that somehow ended upside down, saying to herself, oh, well, that's my humility square.

The whole idea of the humility square makes me a little crazy. Supposedly some Amish lady quilted so perfectly that she needed to intentionally include a mistake in her quilt lest she mock God's perfection. I don't know about you, but mistakes invite themselves into my quilt with no extra effort on my part. And to **intentionally** make a mistake? How humble is that anyway!?

It's possible to do excellent work that is not perfect.
Just remember that perfection is not a reasonable goal.

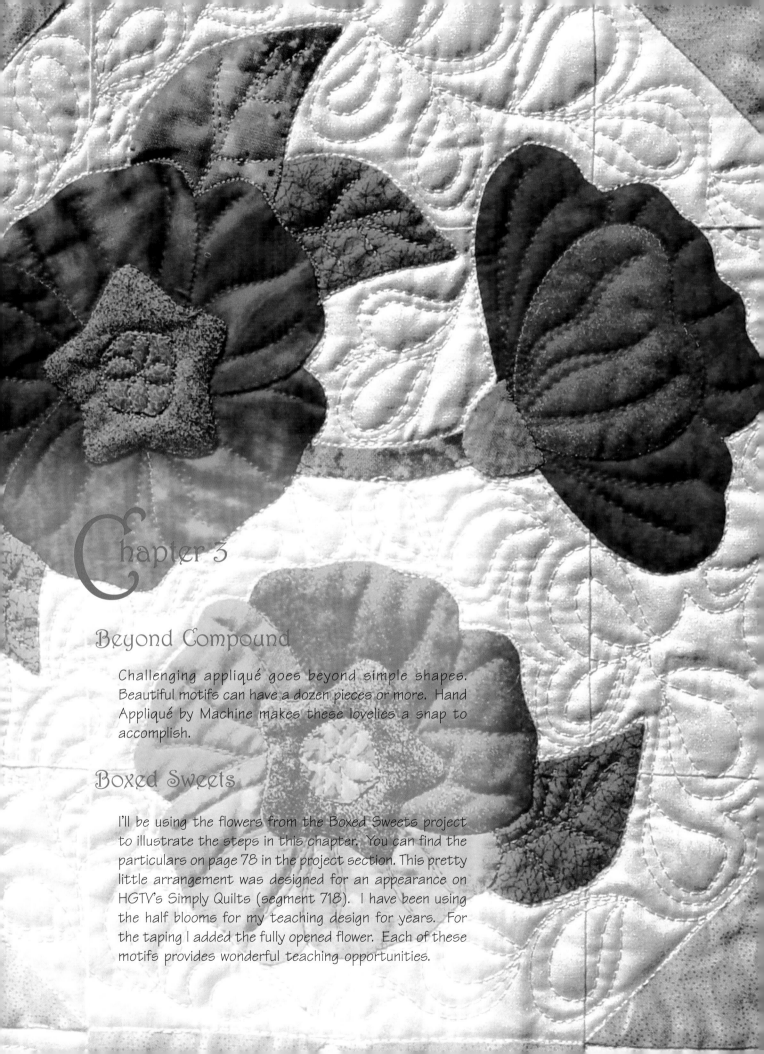

# Chapter 3

## Beyond Compound

Challenging appliqué goes beyond simple shapes. Beautiful motifs can have a dozen pieces or more. Hand Appliqué by Machine makes these lovelies a snap to accomplish.

## Boxed Sweets

I'll be using the flowers from the Boxed Sweets project to illustrate the steps in this chapter. You can find the particulars on page 78 in the project section. This pretty little arrangement was designed for an appearance on HGTV's Simply Quilts (segment 718). I have been using the half blooms for my teaching design for years. For the taping I added the fully opened flower. Each of these motifs provides wonderful teaching opportunities.

## The Half Bloom

We already know all that we need to know to baste the shapes for the half blooms. (We're so smart!) The heart shaped petal in front is totally basted. The side petals are basted on the outside edges, the seam allowance that touches the heart shaped flower becomes an "under". The long petal in the back is basted similarly: the lower edge is an "under", the upper edge an "over." Each of these petals is best basted individually and then docked.

Sometimes bringing all of the pieces together at the base of the flower doesn't go as well as we'd like. The calyx can be basted all the way around and stitched over the messy flower seam allowances.

If the pieces come together beautifully leave the upper edge of the calyx as an "under" and tuck it under the flower. Anytime we do things well we need to show it off to the world!

I always get questions on what fabric to use for the calyx. In some flowers, roses for example, the calyx is formed from the stem, a lovely green swelling at the base of the bloom. In the fuchsia, on the other hand, the calyx is the color of the flower. This flower is not really any flower in particular. I think it sort of looks like a poppy. But it could also be a cosmo or single, old-fashioned rose. In other words, make the calyx whatever color pleases you!

## The Full Bloom

The full bloom offers some excellent new teaching points. We've never dealt with this many similar yet different pieces. Stitching circles on top of other appliqué pieces is also new to us.

The secret to creating these shapes, especially lots of copies of them, is to get organized. Gosh, I know that sounds like punishment. But it's really not like color coding your closet, honest.

# The Key

Way back in Chapter One I suggested that you make extra photocopies of the motifs. I use these as an organizing key. When you're working with more intricate appliqué, a key will save your sanity. The outer petals of our full bloom look an awful lot alike. This can be very frustrating when it comes time to dock the shapes and they don't fit.

To make the key to organize the shapes, we're going label one of the extra photocopies of our motif. Since we already use numbers to designate each layer of freezer paper we are going to use letters to call out each petal.

The process of creating the templates is exactly the same as what we've done in the past until we start cutting the shapes apart. Go ahead and make mirror images. The flower is rather asymmetrical. Mirror images will make the design look more complex. I suggest as you cut the individual shapes apart that you lay that stapled stack of freezer paper shapes down on the key.

For now, just cut the petals away from the star shape. We'll get to the center in a few minutes.

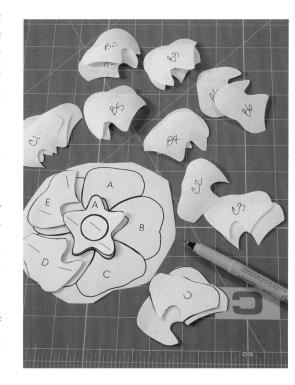

As we remove the staples we need to label each freezer paper layer. Take the staple out of petal A. Toss away the photocopy. Label the first layer of freezer paper A1. The second freezer paper layer would be A2, the third is A3. Got the rhythm?

Likewise, petal B will be B1, B2, B3 and so on. When all of the pieces are labeled gather the shapes into piles of the same number.

As you repeat the process with the other petals (1C, 2C, etc.) stack the petals according to number. You'll end up with six piles of freezer paper templates for complete flowers. When all the templates are in the pile, staple the sets together. One staple now will prevent lost components later. (The closer the deadline the more likely you are to lose a petal.)

Once all of the petals are cut away we are left with a star shape with an irregular circle in the center. Clip through all the paper layers into the star to the center circle. Carefully cut the circle out of the star. Lay the circle and the star onto the key.

Look at the labeled full bloom diagram again. Notice that the arm of the star that protrudes into petal A is also marked with an A. Marking the star shape in this way will make it much easier to get this shape back together again. So as you separate the freezer paper layers of the star shape, label that arm of the star A1, A2, A3, etc.

Finally, remove the staple from the wonky circle. Label the layers. Don't stress over making the circle fit. There's plenty of seam allowance to let you place the circle "close enough".

Remember to staple the sets of freezer paper templates together.

## Adhere the Freezer Paper Templates

Because we have grouped the templates as whole motifs we can now have fun, experimenting with color and value as we choose the fabric for the petals. Play with assigning value to each petal. No worry about which piece goes where, it's time for fun with fabric.

Consider making petals A, B and C dark with D and E assigned to a medium value, for example. Try placing the base of the petal on darker fabric, the outer edge spanning into lighter areas of the fabric. Or, do just the opposite, try dark on the edge and light in the center.

This is the very reason that I make extra freezer paper shapes. I usually experiment with 6 or so sets. I work all the way through pasting and sewing the internal seams until I settle on a couple of color/value combinations that I like. The lessons I learn, the discoveries I make about color and design are well worth a little "wasted" fabric. These motifs end up in my orphaned appliqué tin. They'll find a home someday!

Go ahead and cut the petals from the fabric just as we've done before. The outside edges and those overlapping other petals are all "overs". The parts touching the star or other petals are the "unders". Each petal can be basted individually.

## Dealing with the Clipped Star

The slice in the star template is nothing to worry about. Choose the area of the fabric that you wish to use. Lay the template on that area and press in place, carefully pressing the clipped area first. It doesn't matter if there is a slight space between the edges of the slit. Hand Appliqué by Machine is really very forgiving.

Cut the star from the fabric, adding the seam allowance just as we have in the past. Because the star is relatively small and the curves are rather tight, make the seam allowance a little on the scant side. Clip the seam allowances of the inside curves. Don't cut the hole in the center just yet. Glue baste the entire outside edge of the star.

Clip a hole in the center. Cut the extra fabric away from the center of the star, be sure to leave a ¼" or so seam allowance. This will be the "unders" for the center circle.

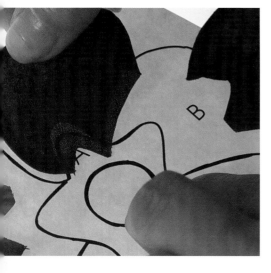

Even though the circle is uneven, don't worry about clipping the curves. Cut the seam allowance a little on the scant size and glue baste. It's really okay if it's not perfect. The "under" seam allowance of the star will cover any character in the circle. Smear the basted circle seam allowance and stick it into the hole in the star.

## Docking the Petals

Place the key on a light box or tape it to a bright window. (It doesn't do much good to use a window at night unless it's summer and you're in Alaska.)

Smear the basted seam allowance of the star freezer paper side up on the illuminated key. Align the labeled arm of the star with the A marking on the key. Work around the star, adding the petals in alphabetical order around the star. The key will help you keep the petals in the right shape. Remember to look through the "under" seam allowances of the petals to dock the shape exactly with the star.

## Stitch & Admire

When all the pieces are in place, carefully flip over your flower and admire your workmanship. Stitch the interior seams. I would start by stitching around the star because that catches the greatest number of pieces. The circle would be stitched next. Finally, go back and catch those little places where the petals overlap each other.

Have fun arranging and rearranging your flowers on the background. Because all the interior seams are sewn it will be very easy to stitch the shapes to the background.

Thinking of how easy all those appliqué designs are going to be now that you know this technique? That would make you my favorite.

# Between the chapters

### Process verses product

I'm not really sure when I crossed the line. I know that when I started quilting it was with a goal in mind. I made my first quilt as a freshman in college. While my buddies were out creating memories to live down I was stitching away in my dorm room, determined to have a full sized evening star quilt for my hope chest. Yes, I had a hope chest in 1975, and yes, my friends thought that I had slipped a cog.

And I finished that quilt in time to smooth it out on the bed in our first apartment. As I closed the door to the bedroom, I was very proud as I glimpsed that quilt, my first quilt, knowing that the next time I saw it I would be a wife.

Of course I had no idea how to quilt. While I hand pieced and hand quilted that first quilt my theory was: the bigger the stitch, the sooner I'm done. I realize now that the quilt was basted together. And as you probably have guessed, that quilt was not long for this world. Which, alas, required the making of quilt #2. This one was a machine pieced, machine quilted (stitched in the ditch) log cabin in browns and oranges. Not long after that quilts followed for the children, baby quilts and then bed quilts.

But somewhere in the middle of all that quilt production I crossed the line. I think it was when my mother-in-law suggested that I put the storm-at-sea quilt I was making for my three-year-old son away until he could appreciate the workmanship. Now if the quilt was the most important part of quilting then storing the quilt away until it could be properly cared for is a reasonable plan.

But at that moment I realized that having a quilt wear out was not a tragedy, it was an opportunity! Dang it all, I'd just have to make another one for him. Gosh, could you please punish me some more?

That was when I surrendered to the process. From that point forward quilts no longer had to have a purpose. I make quilts because I love making quilts. I make big quilts because they take longer. I make small quilts because I want to try something new. I try new fabrics because I want to see how they'll turn out. I try new techniques because I like to be challenged. It's okay to make mistakes because I'll learn something from them.

It's done when I'm done enjoying the process. Life to too short to make work out of our hobbys. If we're not having fun we should be at work!

# Chapter 4

## Bias Stems

There are as many ways to form stems and vines are there are quilters. For example, freezer paper templates were used to make craggy, irregular stems in the No Partridges in This Pear Tree project of Chapter Two.

What follows is my favorite way to make stems. It's not the only way, it's maybe not even the "right" way, but it's the way I like the best.

Part of the beauty of stems in appliqué is the graceful curve. I think of my appliqué as my rebellion. Piecing is very precise, all corners and points. Appliqué can be sinuous, meandering, free flowing and sassy.

## Cutting Bias Strips

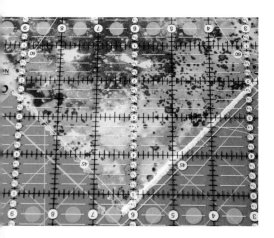

In order to achieve beautiful curves in our stems and vines we need to cut the fabric on the bias grain. I like to cut up fat quarter (18" x 22") sized fabrics for my stems. And, here's a shock; I love to make extra. You never know when you'll need just a couple of inches of stem. I really do have a tin just for leftover stems.

To make bias stems I use a rotary cutter, a 6" x 24" rotary ruler and a self-healing rotary mat.

To begin, press the fabric, deep wrinkles make it harder to cut accurately. Lay the fabric out, single layer, on the self-healing rotary cutting mat.

## Wildly Off Grain

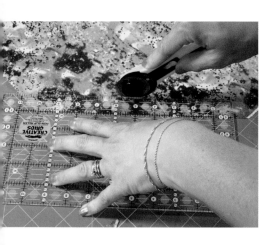

Take a good look at your rotary ruler. Somewhere cris-crossing the ruler you will find a 45° line. Align this line with any straight edge on the fabric. Now don't get nervous about this. We don't need to worry about achieving a perfect bias. The idea is to be wildly off grain. That will get all the flexibility that we need.

Being a cheapskate, I make my first cut towards the lower left hand corner of the fabric, placing the ruler so that the first cut is about 12 inches long. Lefties will start at the lower right hand corner. That gives me a useful length of bias stem and it leaves behind a piece of fabric big enough to sneak out a couple of leaves. Go ahead and make the cut.

Now that we have established the bias with that cut we are going to use our ruler to measure out 1-inch strips. Align the 1" marked line of the rotary ruler with the cut edge of the fabric. As the stems get longer simply cut what you can and then slide the ruler forward to cut the rest of the strip.

The majority of the stems I use are made from bias strips cut 1 inch wide. Occasionally I will cut the strips at ¾" for very fine stems. And ½" bias strips make the tiniest little tendrils.

## Pressing Matters

Next we will press the strips into thirds. Think about how you fold a letter to place in an envelope. Unfortunately green fabrics, the color most likely to end up a bias strip, seem to be especially cranky about holding a pressing. Spray sizing helps to convince them to behave.

Smooth the bias strip out on the ironing board, your iron set at scorch. Generously spray the strip with spray sizing. Fold the top edge down about one third of the way, wrong sides together and press. Be careful only to press the folded portion of the strip. If you press the whole strip at this time you will dry the spray sizing. If you try to spray the strip again to press the other third the first pressing will spring back open.

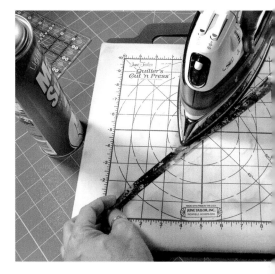

Fold the bottom third up and over the first fold. It should still be damp with spray sizing. Press in place.

Now don't worry about making the bias strip perfectly uniform the entire length. Thick and thin areas can be used to our advantage. Many stems thicken as they form the bud of a flower. This is especially true of roses.

Thin areas can give the illusion of a turn, a twist in a stem, or make a great place for attachment of a leaf.

## Endless yards of bias

Making yards and yards of pressed bias stems gives me design freedom. Yes, I really do snip out the part that best suits me, even if it's right in the middle of a long length. It is a rare occasion when we really do need a long bit of vine. The bias strip is usually interrupted by motifs, flowers, stems, butterflies, vases, etc.

To make very long lengths of bias strips such as we might need for long border vines, join the 1" bias strips, end to end, with a bias seam. Simply overlap the ends of the strips at right angles. Sew from upper left corner to lower right corner. Trim away the excess at the corner, leaving a ¼" seam allowance. Pressing the seams open will reduce the bulk of the seam.

Beth Ferrier

## Placing the Stems

I save the placement of the stems for the last step in the design. I put the flowers, leaves and buds where I want them to be and then "grow" the stem to them. If I have a nice thickening of the strip that I want to take advantage of, I will place that end first. I try to leave at least an inch extra at each of the strip in case a little wandering happens during the stitching process.

To hold the strips down while I stitch, I smear a liberal amount of glue stick on the back of the stem and press it into place. To place the stems in the borders of the Almost Amish quilt (from Chapter 5), I began by tacking down one end of the length of bias. Hold the bias strip with gentle pressure in one hand while the other hand presses it down into place. This is a really easy way to get gentle curves.

Give the glue a chance to dry and then add a few flat flower head pins. The pins are especially helpful when stitching a large piece such as a border. The rustling around, in and out of the machine as we stitch around the shapes can work the stems loose. I try not to use too many pins though. Those babies are sharp and I have a tendency to hurt myself. (Graceful is not usually a word used to describe me.)

## The End is Coming, the end is coming....

We have a couple of options for dealing with the ends of the bias stems and vines. The most obvious is to cover it with something. Usually at least one of the ends of the bias stem is finished with a flower or a leaf. In Winter Roses I made darn sure that the stems were all tucked under something or other.

Another option is run it off the edge. Hey, those flowers have to grow from somewhere! Just try not to go straight into a corner or right into the middle of a side. It's more interesting if you wander off at an odd angle. If your bias strip is headed for a corner, be sure to curve on the way. Unless of course you want an olde timey look, and then straight into the corner is exactly what you should do! (It's your appliqué, who am I to tell you where your stems should go?)

*Hand Applique by Machine*

## The loveliest cut

In My Midnight Garden I could hide the bottom edges of the stems in a gathering of leaves. But the tops of the hollyhocks just had to be naked stem, dang it all. It's a bit of a pain, and you need a little stubborn streak, but it is possible to have a lovely finished edge on the bias stem.

The photos show the steps done using the center motif of Almost Amish.

Cut the folded and pressed bias strip about 3 inches longer than needed. Stitch along the strip, stopping when you get to the point where you would like the stem to end. Leave the sewing machine needle down in the work.

Grab hold of the tail of the bias strip and fold it to the left, turning about a 45° angle. Notice how adjusting this angle gives the end of the stem different shapes. I personally really like a bit of a curve in the angle, but that's a little harder to do. (If anyone could do it, why would I want to?)

Continue stitching along the newly formed angle. Stop about one third of the way from the next point.

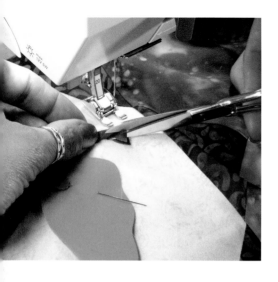

Bring the sewing machine needle up, bring the presser foot up to release the tension on the thread and pull the appliqué towards you.

Carefully trim the excess bias strip. Trim it away at an angle, smaller near the point, larger away from it. If you can, fold back the already stitched area of the stem and snip out a little of the folded edges. This will reduce the bulk in the area and give us some place to sweep away the unfinished edge to.

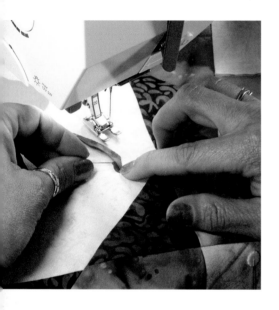

So far, not so bad, eh? This is the stubborn part. Use a heavy-duty quilting pin to pierce the large part of the angle we cut in the bias strip. A seam ripper often works for this job as well. With a curving motion fold this angle under the stem. When nobody's looking it will go perfectly willingly into place. When I demonstrate this for one student it works the first time. When the whole class is watching it gives me fits!

When you've finally had enough and good enough is good enough, stitch to the point, remember to nail that point with a bite right on the end and then stitch down the other side of the stem. If you have a few threads poking out, that's okay. Go ahead and trim them close to the stem. The stitching will hold, I promise!

This is where I always tell the Carnegie Hall joke: A young man, lost on the streets of New York City asks an elderly gentleman for directions. "Sir," he says, "can you tell me how to get to Carnegie Hall?" The old man sighs and says, "practice my son, practice."

Hand Applique by Machine

# Between the chapters
## Sourdough Quilts

Any one who's ever been hoodwinked into accepting a batch of "friendship dough" knows exactly what I'm talking about.

It starts out innocently enough. You visit a good friend. She offers you this marvelous fruit bread with your tea. It's delicious, full of fruit and nuts, spices and a mysterious tangy bite that just entices you to seconds (and thirds).

Your visit is food for the soul. You head for the door, armed with new energy to face the world of bosses and teenagers and deadlines and curfews. It's when you mention one last time the delectable bread that your hostess served that a secret smile passes over her face.

"Come into the kitchen with me. This will only take a minute."

There on the counter are delightfully packaged mason jars of a simple white liquid. A little recipe card dangles seductively from the calico square caught under the golden jar lid ring.

"It's sourdough starter," she says. "Every couple of weeks you stir in some flour and stuff and then you can make these tasty breads for yourself!"

What she doesn't tell you is that sourdough is a living, breathing thing. If you don't feed it, you will feel guilty. If you do feed it, it will grow. It's the only thing I know that grows faster than a teenaged boy. Soon you, too, are looking for unsuspecting friends to introduce to the joys of sourdough. It's the chain letter of the food world.

My fabric stash is like sourdough starter. Every now and then I decide that it's time to use it up. I set to work designing and making quilts that use *tons* of fabric, especially bits and pieces too small to throw out but really not big enough to use.

But I've noticed that no matter how much fabric I already own, every quilt requires at least one shopping trip. It's like feeding the sourdough starter. Soon I find that not only have I made a quilt from my stash, but I have also purchased enough new fabric that I have a great start on the next quilt, and the next!

Good fabric stashes are just like sourdough. They need to be stirred daily. They need to be fed a couple of times a month. And they need to be used for making quilts. But don't worry. You'll never *really* be able to use it up. And it's more fun than sourdough!

# Chapter 5

## Borders, Backgrounds and emBellishments

Appliqué borders add drama and excitement to any quilt, in part because they seem difficult to manage. Of course, we have a few sneaky tricks to make beautiful borders a snap to achieve.

The background for our appliqué is often the plainest piece of muslin we can find. To me that's rather like painting Mona Lisa's head on a garage door. Getting adventurous with your background choices can make your appliqué project stand out from the crowd.

And just because the appliqué is done doesn't mean the quilt is done. We can have some fun with the quilting process to add interest and excitement to our appliqué.

## Border Games

It may seem obvious to some, but if you've never tried to appliqué a border before it may not have occurred to you. It's way easier to appliqué a border before it's sewn to the quilt.

That's pretty much a dope-slap if all of the appliqué is contained within the boundaries of the border fabric. The problems arise when some of the border appliqué wanders into the center piecing or has the gall to wrap around a corner.

It's pretty simple to handle though, if you know a couple of cheap tricks. The Almost Amish quilt was designed to illustrate these strategies. You'll find the particulars in the project section, page 90.

## Into the Center

The flower motifs wander into the triangle blocks of the pieced center in this quilt. They are joined to the border by bias stems. In some cases, the appliqué motifs even span the seam allowances between the center and the borders. The nerve!

To place the appliqué motifs correctly, lay the center block and border strips out where you can work with them easily. For small quilts I use the design wall in my studio. It's only 4 feet wide by 5 feet tall, so that limits the size. For queen sized quilts (my favorite size to make!), I lay the center and borders out on my living room floor. The kids know they'd better walk around it or mom will have a cow. Kelly Cat thinks I put it there for his personal enjoyment. He's so cute that he gets away with it most of the time.

Overlap the borders onto the center by about ½" to simulate the seam allowance. Use glue basting and flat flower head pins to hold the appliqués in place.

Hand Applique by Machine

The pins are important. Quilt borders tend to be larger pieces. The man-handling required to maneuver the fabric through the machine often breaks the glue basting loose. It's especially important to pin where the bias stems meet the flower motifs.

Stitch as much of the appliqué as possible while the quilt is still in pieces. The trick is to stop stitching the appliqués at least ½" from the raw edges of the center and borders. This will allow us to fold back the appliqué to stitch the border seams.

If a shape is completely on the border, but joined to another part by a bias stem, simply leave an opening in the stitching around the shape where the bias stem will enter.

Be sure to leave a few extra inches of bias stem dangling when it needs to span a seam. Sometimes those silly appliqués have a mind of their own and wander off just a bit. (I'm sure that's never happened to you. Having your appliqué wander off, I mean, not you personally mindlessly wandering off. Although I can highly recommend mindlessly wandering off as long as you keep your home in sight.)

When it's time to sew the borders to the quilt, gently fold the appliqué out of the way. It's not always necessary to pin the shapes out of the way of the seam. The larger the piece I'm working on, the more likely I am to use pins.

Sew the seams one at a time, (obviously), and finish the appliqué around that seam before sewing the next seam. That way you only have to wrestle with the entire quilt for the last border.

# Dare to be Odd

It's a natural tendency to want to balance design at the center and corners of the quilt's borders. While repetition is often beautiful and comforting, it can also be incredibly boring!

The Almost Amish quilt's border design repeats around the quilt. It even repeats four times, the same way on each border. But it's not centered on each side; the repeat spans the corner. That forces the viewer to spend a little time trying to figure out what's up with the border pattern. It's very good to confuse the viewer.

In my Clumsy Gardener (available as a pattern) quilt the border appliqué is balanced in opposite corners, but the appliqué is of different lengths.

And in My Celestial Garden (also available as a pattern) the appliqué is centered on each side. That looks pretty silly when the quilt is flat on the wall. But I have a four poster bed. If I put the appliqué in the corners it would have been lost. I think appliqué is to be admired. I really like coming up the stairs and seeing my beautiful appliqué showcased at the foot of the bed.

And I have an attitude problem about pillow tucks. I just hate it when the top border disappears into the tuck under the pillows. It looks for all the world to me like the quilt is having a wedgie.

I like to create a similar, but different border for pillow end of a bed quilt. I often add a 12" pillow tuck border to the top edge of my bed quilts. The side border appliqués are just stretched out a bit to make up the difference in the length. We can do this easily because the interior seams of our appliqués are already done! If you're going to put a quilt on a bed it should fit well, eh?

# Background Check

Does your appliqué suffer from boring background syndrome? Choosing interesting fabrics and treatments for the background for your appliqué won't overwhelm it; it will keep the viewer interested.

## To Piece or Not to Piece

A simple way to add excitement to your project is to use background fabric with a little personality. It doesn't have to shout at you, a subtle print will do.

Every now and then a fabric manufacturer will bring out a print that screams "appliqué me!" I buy lots of yards of that. Several of the designs in this book have backgrounds of just such a fabric. It was called Fairy Frost, done by Michael Miller and I bought tons of it in several colorways! I think it's interesting without being intrusive. And it's sparkly. I like sparkly.

If the background fabric is a 12-inch square, or larger, then I want to piece it. When it comes to fabric, less is NOT more, less is just less. Fully half of my fabric stash is made up of 1-yard cuts of potential background fabrics.

If a design calls for a 12" background square, I'm likely to make a four-patch (cut 6 ½" squares) or even a nine-patch (cut 4 ½" squares). It's just more interesting!

Four-patches are great for large, bed-sized quilts. A nine-patch would be better for smaller wallhangings. It's a matter of scale. If the pieces are too small for the project the background could become tedious and distracting.

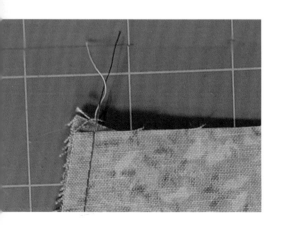

For the Midnight Garden and Winter Roses quilts, I decided to use add sashings between the background blocks to give the illusion of a trellis. The design used only two different background fabrics, but added lots of interest.

Divide the finished block size by 3 or 4 to determine a pleasant width for the sashing. One-third or one-quarter width sashings make a comforting proportion without overwhelming the block.

## Stack and Slash

One of my favorite appliqué backgrounds is "Stack and Slash". It's mindless to create. It gives the appliqué background the look of old china.

We will need one background fabric square for each finished "Stack and Slash" we desire. We also will need a rotary cutter, a 6" x 24" ruler and self-healing mat.

Neatly stack the fabric squares, all right side up. Make stacks of no more than 8 layers of fabric, it's too hard to cut more than that at one time. More fabrics will make more interesting blocks; a minimum of six different fabrics is suggested. Evenly distribute the fabrics into the piles.

Work all the steps on one stack first, and then repeat all the steps on the next stack of squares.

Lay the 6" x 24" ruler on top of the stack on an angle. The top corner of the stack should be at **about** 2 inches from the cutting edge of the ruler; the bottom corner should be at **about** 3 ½" from the edge.

Cut through all six layers.

Take the stack to the sewing machine. Take the top fabric off the smaller angle pile, move it to the bottom of the stack. Sew the pieces back together, right sides together. Be sure to off set the ends slightly. Press the seams towards the smaller piece.

Stack the six blocks again, alternating the smaller pieced angle between top and bottom. They are shown spread out here so that you can see the way to alternate the block. Your stack will be right on top of each other.

Now cut again, this time 2 inches from the top corner and 3 inches from the bottom corner. Now take the top two of the smaller angle and shuffle them to the bottom of the stack. Sew the angles back together, offsetting as above. Press the seams toward the smaller angle. Square the blocks to desired size.

Now repeat the steps with the rest of your fabric squares. Start with a fabric square about 1 ½ inch larger than the desired finished size.

## Look to the Stars

Some of the most beautiful appliqué quilts that I have ever seen have used complex pieced blocks for background. Use subtle shadings in star blocks to create spectacular backgrounds.

The hardest thing about using pieced blocks for background is covering our perfect piecing with appliqué. It totally goes against every fiber of my being to appliqué over perfect points. Luckily my points aren't perfect so often as to cause much of a problem.

Working with finished motifs lets me move that appliqué over just enough to show off that excellent star point allowing me to prove that occasionally I can make star points that would make the quilt police proud.

## Gilding the Lily

When it comes to the quilting of our appliqué we have the opportunity to enhance the design. Consider using a closely stitched pattern in the background around the appliqué. More stitching causes an area to recede.

A stitched grid around an appliqué is especially lovely. The regimen of stitched lines around the curves of the appliqué make a beautiful counterpoint.

Plan to stitch in the ditch near the edge of the appliqué shapes. This line of stitching encourages the edge of the appliqué to roll just a bit completely hiding our machine stitches. You really will have people arguing with you about how it was done!

## Bobbin Work

Stitching in the ditch also serves as a road map for bobbin work. Quilters like to make it seem mysterious, but bobbin work is simply quilting from the wrong side. It allows us to use threads for quilting that won't cooperate in the needle. I like to use bobbin work to add details like tendrils and veins.

## And the bead goes on

Beading on quilts is something that I am just starting to explore. I have enjoyed adding the occasional bead to the tips of my leaves and edges of petals to suggest drops of dew.

While back in my silk ribbon by machine phase I did stitch beads on by machine, when adding just a few beads widely spaced, a hand needle and neutral thread works just fine for me.

The Projects

## General Directions

The specific directions for each of the projects can be found in the following pages. The directions assume that you have a basic knowledge of rotary cutting and machine piecing.

Unless otherwise noted, a 1/4-inch seam allowance is used in the piecing through out. Please take the time to be sure that your seam allowances are accurate.

## Rotary Cutters

All the directions are written for rotary cutting. Please be sure to use a good quality cutter, and don't scrimp on blades. The sharper the blade, the easier it is to cut accurately.

Be careful with the cutter. Never, never, ever put the rotary cutter down open. Be sure to latch it closed each time it leaves your hand. These blades are really sharp and a trip to the emergency room really cuts into your quilting time! And should you have the misfortune of bleeding on your quilt then you must also spit on it. The enzymes in your saliva will dissolve your blood before it stains. Spitting on someone else's blood on your quilt might make you feel better, but it won't remove the stain.

## Blah, blah, blah

And even though I know you think it's a pain, be sure to read **all the way through** each pattern before you sew.

## It's my story and I'm sticking with it.

The directions for each project include full size templates for each of the motifs.

The directions do NOT include full size layout diagrams. There's a good reason for that.

One of the most rewarding aspect of this technique is the flexiblity that comes with finished motifs. No longer do we have to live in fear of missed marks on the background or shapes that didn't overlap properly.

One of the things that sucks the joy out of applique for me is the focus on recreating designs EXACTLY as if that means they have been rendered *perfectly*.

In my humble opinion the last thing we need is more stress, especially in our hobbies.

So if you want to copy my layouts exactly that's okay with me, in fact, I would be honored to know that you liked them that well. Just take the layout diagrams to the office supply store and enlarge them.

## Block Placement

Take a little time with arranging your finished appliqué. We made all those extra motifs so that we can play with the placement. Start by laying out the background in a place that you can get back away from it. I like to lay my quilts out on the living room floor. I can then go partway up the stairs and look down on the design. Toss the appliqué motifs on the background in the general positions of the design. Don't spend a lot of time on it just yet.

I take a cup of tea with me, have a seat on the steps and just look at the quilt. Don't work at it; just let your eyes wander over the colors. After a few minutes I can see which motifs have the most character, the attention seekers.

Resist the urge to place the strong or dark motifs in the corners, or balanced in the centers of each side, or even right in the center. When the attention getting appliqués are balanced they act like a prison for the rest of the quilt. They literally stop the eye.

Anytime there is a pattern to the placement it makes the design less interesting. Keeping the balance a little off kilter confuses the eye; it entices the viewer to keep exploring the quilt. That is what we want!

# Five of Hearts

Finishes about 18" square

## Supply List

Appliqué tools as outlined in Chapter One
1 ¼" sticky label circle recommended for the center circle

## Fabric:

5" square of fabric for each heart
2"x 4" rectangle of fabric for each leaf
2" square of fabric for the center circle
16"-18" square of fabric for background

To make one Five of Heart wreath you will need just one photocopy of the templates on page 73. You will need a few more photocopies if you decide to make a queen sized quilt version (remember to send me a picture!)

Hand Applique by Machine

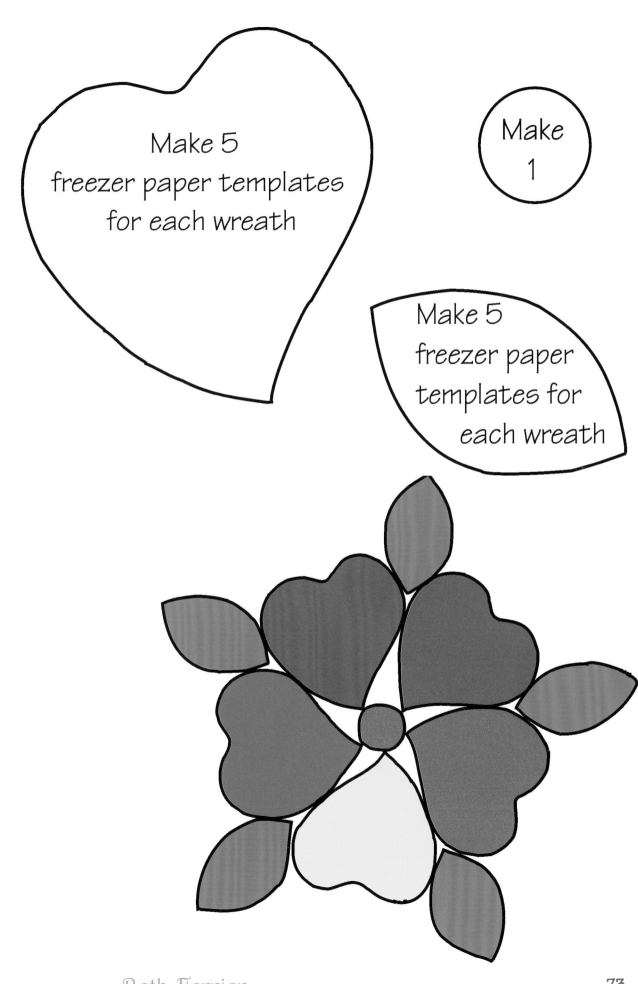

Make 5
freezer paper templates
for each wreath

Make
1

Make 5
freezer paper
templates for
each wreath

# No Partridge in This Pear Tree

Finished size: 28" wide by 39" long

## Supply List

Appliqué notions as described in Chapters One and Two

## Fabric:

Twenty-four 6" squares of black fabric for background
½ yard black fabric for border
1/3 yard gold and silver fabric for binding
Dark, medium and light gold metallic print fat quarters (18"x22") for pears and vase
Dark, medium and light silver metallic print fat quarters (18"x22") for leaves
Two medium browns with gold print for trunks

To make your quilt just like mine you will need freezer paper templates for 9 pears and 16 leaves. You know me; I'd be making twelve pears and at least 18 leaves. Remember that we can cut up to 6 layers of freezer paper at one time and I like to make extra motifs so that I can play with color and value on the design.

The trunks of the topiary were made with freezer paper templates. (Yes, I could have made them with bias strips, but I didn't want to teach you about bias strips in this project and I wanted a sort of craggy look anyway!) Glue baste all of the long sides of both stems. Weave the pieces together and then stitch the "overs".

For the vase, the center section side seams were the "overs", glue baste those first. Dock the center with the two side templates and then glue baste the whole vase.

Basting and docking the small segments to the large segments created the corner motifs. The outside edges were then basted and finally, the diagonal line was then basted and docked.

# Finishing touches

The background for my sample was made of twenty-four 5 ½" (finished size) blocks (4 wide by 6 high) of black fabric that was stacked and slashed. Start with 7 ½" squares of fabric. (Please refer to Chapter 5 for directions for stack and slash blocks and lots of other choices for making your appliqué backgrounds more interesting.) The border is 3" wide (3 ½" raw size). I usually cut my bindings 2" wide. For this quilt I cut the binding strips on the bias to take advantage of the stripe in the fabric.

Leaf

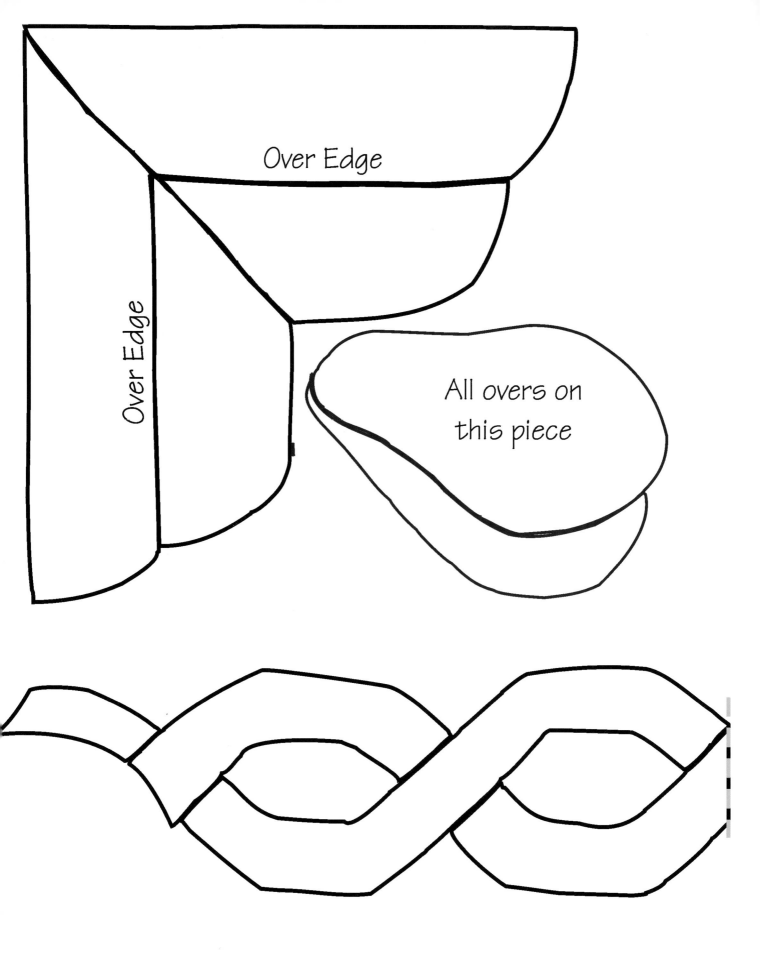

Over Edge

Over Edge

All overs on
this piece

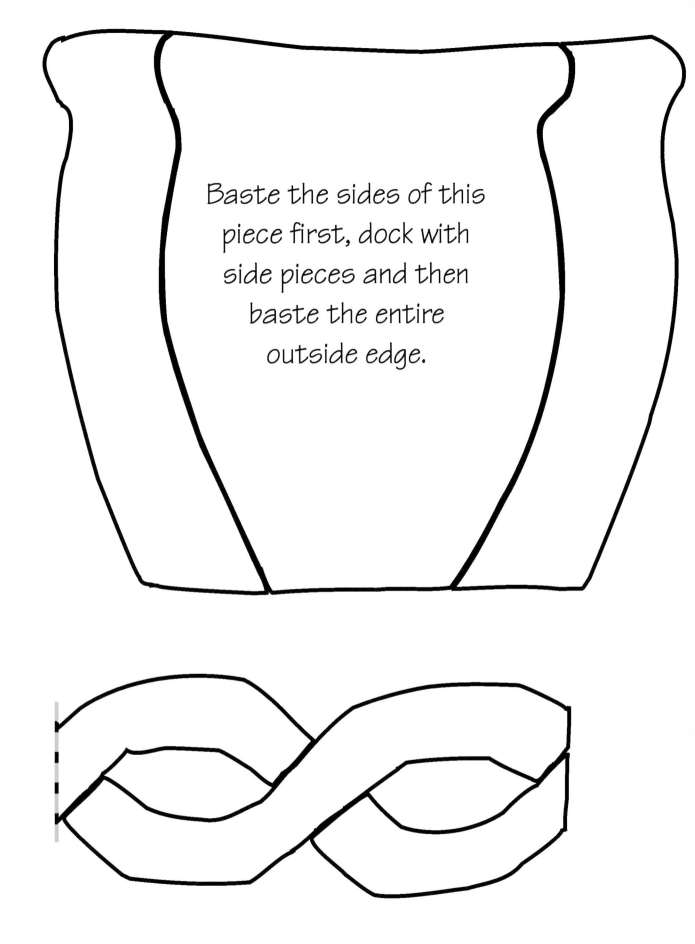

Baste the sides of this piece first, dock with side pieces and then baste the entire outside edge.

# Boxed Sweets

Finished size: 36" square

## Supply List

Appliqué notions

## Fabric:

Assortment of flower fabric, include values dark to light
Fabric for center circle, center star, stems and leaves.

**1 yard Background fabric**
Cut one strip 7 ¼" x Width of Fabric
      Cut four 7 ¼" squares
      Cut one 6 ½" square
Cut three strips 6 ½" x width of fabric
      Cut three 6 ½" squares
      Cut thirty-two 6 ½" x 3 ½" rectangles.
      Cut eight 3 7/8" squares,
            cut each of these on the diagonal once.
Cut one strip to 3 ½" x width of fabric.
      Cut sixteen 3 ½" squares

**½ yard Accent fabric**
Cut three strips 3 7/8" x width of fabric.
      Cut twenty-four 3 7/8" squares. **Draw** a diagonal line on the wrong side of sixteen of the squares. **Cut** eight of the squares on the diagonal once.

**¼ yard Binding Fabric**
Cut four strips 2" x width of fabric.

## To piece the background squares

This is just the slickest trick! Start with the 7 ¼" background squares and the 3 7/8" accent fabric squares with the line drawn on the wrong side.

Layer two 3 7/8" dark squares and the 7 ¼" background square right sides together. The squares are on opposite corners of the block. Stitch ¼" on both sides of the line. Cut on the line and press the seam towards the small squares. See the heart shape?

Hand Applique by Machine

Now lay another 3 7/8" square right sides together on the remaining corner of the background square. The drawn diagonal line should go from the corner through the small triangles. Stitch ¼" on both sides of the line.

Repeat this with the last square and the other heart shape. Cut on the line and press towards the small square. Viola! Flying geese!

Sew the triangles cut from the 3 7/8" squares together to make sixteen half-square triangles of background and accent fabric.

Sew a background square to each of the half-square triangles. Make sure to sew it to the accent triangle.

Sew a 6 ½" rectangle to the unit we just made and the flying geese we made earlier.

These pieces become a fancy nine-patch background for our quilt. Appliqué the motifs before sewing the blocks together.

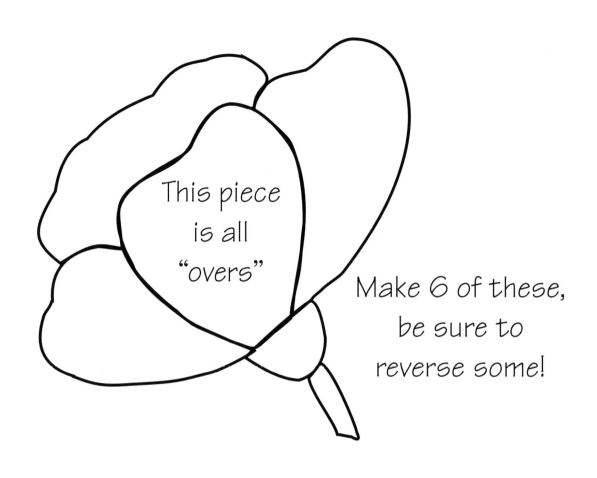

This piece is all "overs"

Make 6 of these, be sure to reverse some!

Make 8 and 8 reversed

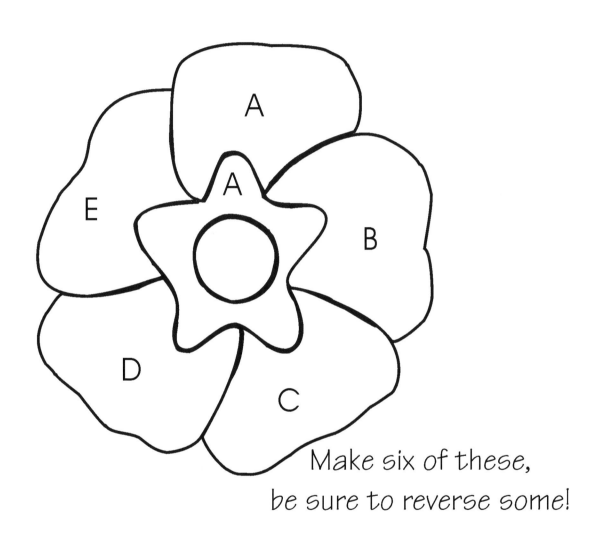

Make six of these,
be sure to reverse some!

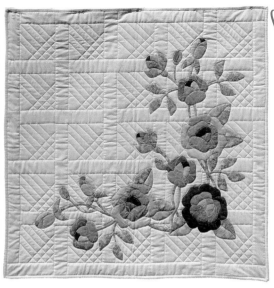

# Winter Roses

Finished size: 30" square

**Appliqué fabrics:** Fat quarters (18" x 22") of 6 to 8 blue fabric in values from light to dark.

**1 yard Background fabric:**

Cut twenty-five 4 ¾" squares

also cut four 2" strips for binding

**¾ yard Background Trellis fabric:**

Cut two strips 6 ¼" x width of fabric

Cut thirty-four 2" x 6 ¼" rectangles

Cut two strips 4 ¾" wide

Cut twenty-five 2" x 4 ¾" rectangles

From the remainder cut one 2" x 7 ½" rectangle

## Piece the Background

Sew a 2" x 4 ¾" rectangle to each of the squares. Press all of the seams towards the trellis rectangles.

Turn the block so that the trellis strip is on the bottom. Sew a 2" x 6 ¼" rectangle to the left side of each of the squares.

To five of these blocks, sew a 2" x 6 ¼" rectangle to the top of the block (the side opposite the first rectangle).

To one of these blocks sew the 2" x 7 ½" rectangle to the right side of the block. This will make a block with trellis rectangles on all sides. This block goes in the upper right hand corner of the background.

Put these five blocks aside, they will become the top row of the background.

To four more of the blocks sew a 2" x 6 ¼" rectangle to the right side (opposite the second rectangle) of the block. These will form the right column of the background.

## The Appliqué

The wider stems are 1" bias strips. The narrow stems were cut at ¾". Be sure to make mirror image freezer paper template of the small leaf.

## The Quilting

I quilted diagonal lines in the background squares to suggest a shadow cast by the trellis. The partial grid stitches were done with a pale gray thread.

Stitch in the ditch around the trellis rectangles to suggest that the strips are woven together.

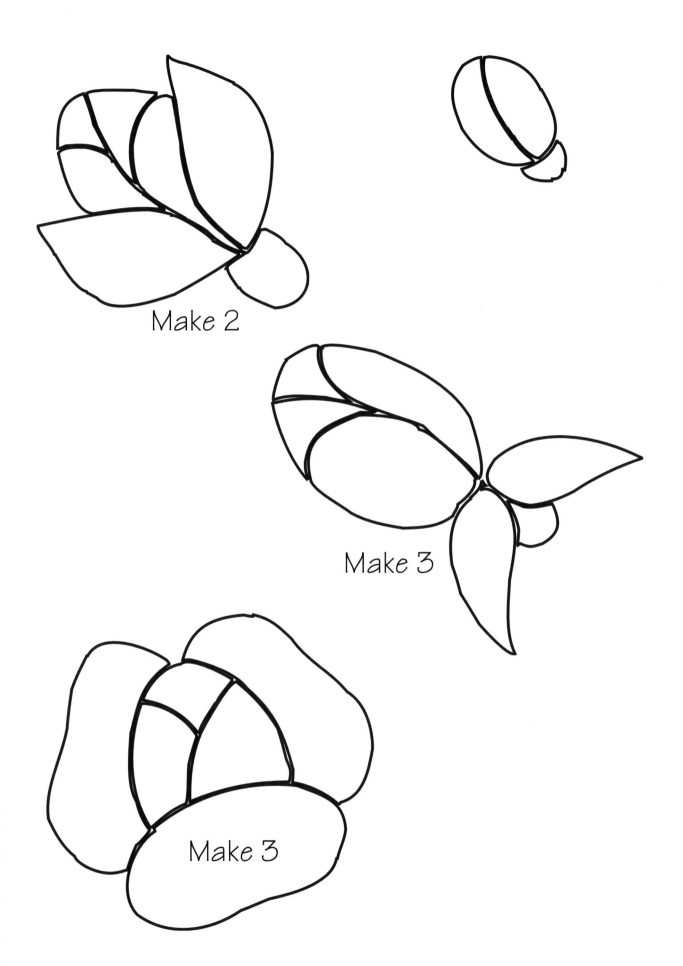

Make 2

Make 3

Make 3

Make
6

Make 3

Make
14

# Midnight in the Garden

Finished size: 18" square

**Appliqué fabrics:** small amounts of purple and pinks for the fucshias, reds for small flowers, three shades of blue for the hollyhocks, several greens for stems and leaves.

½ yard **Background fabric:** Cut nine 6" squares
    also cut two 2" strips for binding
¼ yard **Background Sashing fabric:**
Cut a strip 7 ½" x width of fabric
    Cut four 7 ½" x 2" rectangles
Cut the remainder of the strip to 6" wide
    Cut eight 2" x 6" rectangles

## Piece the Background

Sew a 2" x 6" rectangle to eight of the squares.

Sew a 2" x 7 ½" rectangle to four of these squares.

Yes you *should* have one square left! That belongs in the lower left-hand corner.

## The Appliqué

The stems for the fuchsias are ½" bias strips. Cut those from the desired green fabric first, then cut the appliquéd leaves from the scraps.

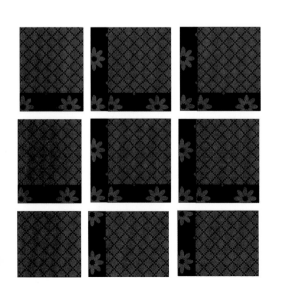

The stems for the hollyhocks are 1" bias strips.

Hand Applique by Machine

Make 3

Make 3

Make 4
of these

Make 4
and 3 reversed

Make one and
one reversed

I made just
one of these

# Hollyhock Templates

Make 4

Make 2
of these guys

Make 4

Make 2
and 2 reversed
Make one with
no center division.

Make 2

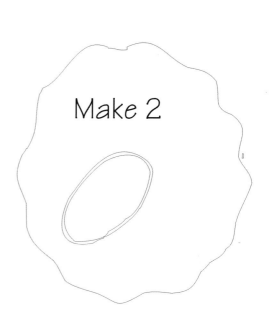

# Almost Amish

Finishes 36" square

The appliqué fabric came from gradated 1/8 yard cut collections of hand-dyed fabric from Caryl Bryer Fallert's studio. See resources for contact information.

The stems are 1" wide bias strips cut from the remainder of the Star Point fabric. Cut 8 strips on the diagonal across the full width of the strip for the border vines. The center motif strip can come from the corner, it won't need to be as long.

The circles are cut from the leftover Accent fabric.

**½ yard Background fabric:** Cut one 11 ¼" square, cut on the diagonal twice to make four triangles.
Cut one 10 ½" square; cut sixteen 4" squares.
**1/3 yard Star Point fabric:** Cut two 11 ¼" squares, cut on the diagonal twice to make four triangles.
**1/3 yard Accent fabric:** Cut one 11 ¼" square, cut on the diagonal twice to make four triangles.
Cut four 3 3/8" squares; mark the diagonal on the wrong side of each block.
**1 yard Border fabric:** Cut four 7 ½" x 24 ½" rectangles
Cut sixteen 4" squares

Start with the 10 ½" background square and the 3 3/8" accent fabric squares. Align the small squares with the corners of the background block. The diagonal line you drew should cut across the corner. Stitch; cut away the corner leaving a ¼" seam allowance. Press the seam towards the small triangle.

Use the triangles from the 11 ¼" squares to make an hourglass block. Press the seams towards the accent fabric triangle. Finally, when the blocks are sewn, trim the hourglass block to 7 ½" x 10 ½", trimming away part of the accent triangle.

Use the 4" background and border squares to make eight four-patches.

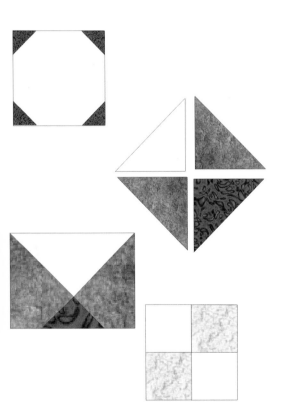

Hand Appliqué by Machine

Complete the block. The seams of the light triangles should crisscross ¼" below the raw edge. That will give you those perfect points that the quilt police are looking for! Another nine-patch, imagine that!

Sew a four-patch to each end of two of the border rectangles. Appliqué the borders following the directions in Chapter 5.

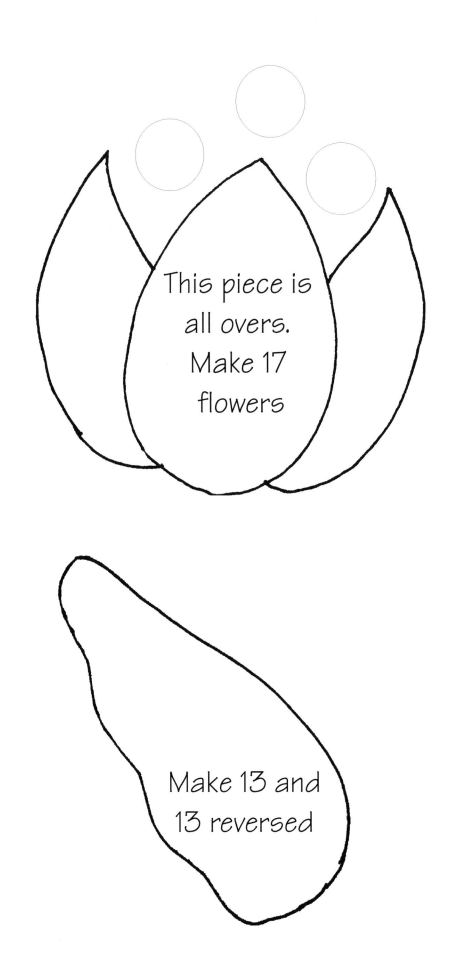

This piece is
all overs.
Make 17
flowers

Make 13 and
13 reversed

# And Now a Few Words From Our Sponsors

For even more quilting fun try our first book,

## Out of the Cupboard and Onto the Bed
## Practically Free Quilts from your Fabric Stash

You'll find easy to follow instructions for 6 quilts to cover every bed and use up some of your stash of fabric. Forty pages of fun and excellent directions with over 100 diagrams and full color photographs of each quilt.

### At Home in My Heart

Six charmingly simple quilts are designed to teach valuable quilting skills as well as brighten your home. This uplifting book contains twenty-four pages of excellent fun, complete instructions for piecing and applique for twin, double and queen size bed quilts plus two wall hangings and a cozy lap quilt. Beautiful full color photographs of each quilt.

Designed in honor and rememberance of the everyday heros of 9/11/01.

We're a family owned and operated business. Kent has a real job during the day. In his spare time he does the web page work, photography and typesetting for the books.

The boys work in the office, folding and stuffing patterns, filing paperwork. They also haul beds around the yard for photography when Mom asks.

Beth gets to work at sewing, designing, writing, teaching and traveling. Quilting **is** her day job! If you would like to have Beth come and play with your guild or at your local quilt shop, please contact us.

You can find a full listing of her lecture and workshop offerings on the website. Or you can actually call us. The phone number is in the front of the book.

## Applewood Farm Publications also has a whole slew of patterns that you

might like to try. Many of the patterns are designed especially for teaching patchwork techniques. We even have teaching guides for each title to make using the patterns for classes as easy as pie. There is always fun stuff on the web page. Check us out at:

## www.applewoodfarmquilts.com

# Index

# Resources

The very best place to find excellent materials for your all of your quilting needs is your local quilt shop.  Running a quilt shop is very hard work and often a thankless job.  Buying something is the best way to thank them for being there.

For those of you not lucky enough to have a local quilt shop these fine people can help you find cool stuff to use in your projects.

For the finest of invisble threads and excellent decorative threads for quilting:
Sulky of America
www.sulky.com
asksulky@aol.com

To find a local dealer of the best sewing machines on the planet:
Bernina of America
3702 Prarie Lake Court
Aurora, IL 60504
630-978-2500
www.berninausa.com

The incredible fabric used in the Almost Amish applique motifs was made by:
Caryl Bryer Fallert
Bryerpatch Studio
www.bryerpatch.com

# The Last Word

I just don't see why it's such a big deal to finish something. Whenever I lecture at guilds the subject of UFO's (UnFinished Objects) always seems to come up. Okay, so I bring it up. I have so many UFO's that they have categories. I see nothing wrong with this.

When my kids were little I finished each project before I started another. I was a full-time stay-at-home mom. With four little hyperactive boys chasing through the house you can be sure that I was pretty busy with chores. By the end of some days it was hard to tell that I had done anything at all; the dishes had been cleaned and dirtied several times over, the laundry was done, until they dressed for bed; and don't even talk to me about the bathroom I just cleaned!

My quilting was the only thing I did that stayed done. Taking that last stitch in the binding let me feel a real sense of accomplishment. My quilts were something that no frecklefaced little boy could undo.

Now the boys are almost grown. Two of them are off to college, leaving two at home. They do the lion's share of the household chores around here. They make the messes and besides I'm trying to raise boys that a wife will thank me for someday. It is a real hoot to hear them bellow about the mess someone else makes of their freshly mopped floor.

My quilts have become my spirit's voice. In many ways, they are like children to me. You can't hurry them along any more than you can a dawdling two-year-old. If you try, the process just becomes a miserable battle of wills.

Some quilts need to age. That fabulous fabric will come back into style any time now. Some quilts haven't decided what they want to be when they grow up. For other quilts I haven't learned what I need to know to properly finish them yet. You know, if we finish them all what treasures will our grandchildren have to discover in the antiques shops?

Done is a four-letter word, finish is an "f-word". They have been banished from my quilting vocabulary.

Quilt projects are like fine wines, they need to mature. And so do I, but I'm not in any hurry to do that either.